CONTENTS

LEONARDO DA VINCI

YOUNG ARTIST, WRITER, AND INVENTOR

by George E. Stanley

Aladdin Paperbacks

New York   London   Toronto   Sydney

❧ ALADDIN PAPERBACKS
An imprint of Simon & Schuster Children's Publishing Division
1230 Avenue of the Americas, New York, NY 10020
Text copyright © 2005 by George E. Stanley
All rights reserved, including the right of reproduction in whole or in part in any form.
ALADDIN PAPERBACKS, CHILDHOOD OF WORLD FIGURES, and colophon are trademarks of Simon & Schuster, Inc.
Designed by Lisa Vega
The text of this book was set in Aldine 721.
Manufactured in the United States of America
First Aladdin Paperbacks edition October 2005
10 9 8 7 6
Library of Congress Control Number 2004118395
ISBN 13: 978-1-4169-0570-7
ISBN-10: 1-4169-0570-7
1209 OFF

LEONARDO
DA VINCI

CHAPTER ONE
A GENIUS IS BORN

It was a glorious day in the middle of May 1452. From the kitchen window Caterina could watch her baby Leonardo's cradle in the grass.

For some reason, Caterina told everyone, Leonardo was happier when he was outdoors in the sunshine. If Leonardo cried, and if he wasn't hungry or if his diaper wasn't wet, then all Caterina had to do was put him in his cradle and take him outside. Leonardo could stay there for hours. Caterina wasn't exactly sure what it was that interested Leonardo. It could have been the shapes of the clouds. It could have been the birds flying above him. Soon, Caterina was sure, when Leonardo started to talk, he would tell her.

Suddenly, Caterina screamed. A large hawk had just landed on Leonardo's cradle. The pitcher she had been holding fell from her hands and shattered on the stone floor.

Carterina dashed for the door and ran as fast as she could toward her baby. If she didn't hurry, she knew, the hawk would pick up Leonardo with its sharp talons and carry him back to its lair in the nearby mountains.

Caterina had heard stories of that happening. She had even seen hawks do it with small animals.

Caterina's heart was beating wildly, and she was finding it difficult to breathe. As she neared the cradle, she started clapping her hands and shouting, hoping to scare off the bird before it could take her baby.

The hawk wasn't moving, though. It didn't seem to be afraid of her at all. That wasn't good. She had heard that, too. The hawks were getting braver and braver, the people in the village of Vinci said.

Right before Caterina reached the cradle,

she suddenly stopped, hardly believing what she was seeing. It wasn't a real hawk at all. It was a hawk *kite* that had landed on top of Leonardo.

"My baby, you must be terrified," Caterina said.

Once again, Caterina had a surprise: Leonardo was actually smiling. As Caterina lifted the kite away from Leonardo, he raised his hands as if to stop her.

With Leonardo in her arms, Caterina sat on the soft green grass beside the cradle and rocked her son back and forth.

"You are such a beautiful baby," Caterina whispered to Leonardo. "You are a joy to me and your father."

Although Caterina had not married Ser Piero, Leonardo's father, together they shared in the excitement of having a son whom they were both sure would be very special when he grew up.

Caterina loved Ser Piero, but she was only a peasant, and he was a member of one of the more important families in Vinci. She accepted her fate. That was simply the way things were, and Caterina felt no bitterness toward anyone. *How could I?* she thought as she looked at Leonardo's smiling face.

Ser Piero's parents, Antonio and Monna Lucia, adored their new grandchild and showered him with love and affection. Caterina knew they didn't have to do that. But Leonardo's grandfather often broke with tradition. His family had always been notaries, men of the law, and had made names for themselves in Rome. But Antonio wanted to lead a quieter life, so he had chosen to run the family estate in Vinci. The arrival of their first grandson, even though his birth was not legitimate and his mother was not of their social status, was a very happy event. They were both elderly, and they had almost given up on having any grandchildren.

Antonio proudly recorded Leonardo's birth in the family papers, making sure there were plenty of friends and family members at

Leonardo's baptism. He told everyone he came in contact with that he accepted Leonardo as a member of the family. Ser Piero's brother, Francesco, was delighted to be an uncle and was constantly telling Caterina about all of the things he planned to teach his nephew.

Caterina knew that if Ser Piero had been more like his father, Antonio, or even his brother Francesco, then they might have eventually married. After all, even though she belonged to the peasant class, her beauty had caused more than one Italian gentleman to look twice. But it was in Ser Piero's blood to continue the family tradition of law. A marriage to Caterina was not in his plans.

"With Ser Piero away so often on business, Father has said that I'll soon be running the estate," Francesco told Caterina one day. "When Leonardo is old enough to walk, I want to show him everything his family owns."

"I think Leonardo would like that very much, Francesco," Caterina said.

At the time, Caterina wondered if that

meant Antonio would eventually acknowledge Leonardo legally as his grandson, making him an heir. But over the next few months it became evident that, while the entire family adored Leonardo and treated him as a member of the family, Leonardo would never be in line to inherit any of the family's fortune.

Caterina decided she shouldn't be overly concerned about that, though. Something in her heart told her that Leonardo would not only succeed in life without this legal recognition but that he would become famous all over the world.

When Caterina said as much to members of her own family, they didn't make fun of her for thinking this. In fact, several of them nodded and said, "A mother knows these things."

Even though Antonio and Monna Lucia lived nearby, because of their age, it was getting harder and harder for them to come by to see Leonardo. Caterina could see the sadness in their eyes each time they left him.

Francesco also visited several times a day.

When Leonardo took his first steps, Francesco jumped up and down and gleefully announced that Leonardo was now ready to walk around the estate with him.

Caterina laughed. "Francesco! Francesco! You are so impatient!" she said. "Leonardo would soon tire, and you would end up having to carry him most of the way."

Francesco picked Leonardo up and hugged him. "Oh, I wouldn't mind that at all, Caterina," he said. "I would do anything for my nephew."

Later, Caterina believed that that was the moment she made a very important decision: When Leonardo was weaned, she would take him to Ser Piero's family. Caterina knew how much they wanted this, and she knew, too, that they could give him a much better life than she ever could. So, in 1454, when Leonardo was two years old, he went to live with Antonio and Monna Lucia.

As Caterina was leaving her son, she felt the tears welling up in her eyes. She suddenly wondered if she was doing the right thing, but Leonardo gave her a big smile and waved good-bye, then he took his uncle Francesco's hand and together they headed off for a tour of the estate.

"He is in very good hands, Caterina," Antonio said. "Francesco is not good at many things, but he does love the land, and he does love Leonardo."

Caterina nodded. "I know," she whispered. "I know."

"Go on back home now, dear. Your work in the fields is waiting for you," Monna Lucia said. "But always remember what happiness you have brought to this old couple."

Caterina left Antonio and Monna Lucia's house, but she stopped once more, midway to her small house, to watch Francesco and Leonardo as they neared one of the olive groves.

Suddenly, Leonardo stopped and turned. He waved at Caterina.

Caterina waved back.

Francesco said something, and Leonardo turned to look at one of the trees.

Caterina knew that Antonio and Monna Lucia would welcome her anytime she wanted to visit Leonardo, but in her heart she knew that his new life had begun and that the role she was meant to play in her son's life was over.

Francesco and Leonardo were now in the middle of the olive grove, and Francesco was talking to his nephew as if he were a merchant from Florence or Siena or even Rome.

"As you can see, Leonardo, I have just recently pruned these trees," Francesco said. "It's warm enough now, that any growth won't be killed by—"

Leonardo had reached for one of the fruiting branches of olives.

"No, you mustn't eat them now, Leonardo," Francesco said hurriedly. "They're quite bitter!"

"I only want to touch them," Leonardo told his uncle.

Francesco watched as Leonardo's fingers

played gently with the branch, the leaves, and finally with the fruit itself. Then, without saying a word, Leonardo looked around until he found a small, pointed stick on the ground.

To Francesco's absolute amazement, Leonardo used the stick to draw a picture of the hanging olives in the soft soil beneath the tree.

When Leonardo was finished, Francesco dropped to his knees and inspected what Leonardo had done. "They look so real, I could probably sell these olives to some merchant," Francesco said with a smile.

Leonardo thought that was funny and laughed.

"There are people in Vinci who called themselves artists who cannot draw this well, Leonardo," Francesco said in a serious tone. "How did you do this?"

Leonardo shrugged. "I don't know, Uncle," he said. "I just did."

Francesco stood up. "Well, let's see what else you can draw, then," he said.

They went next to the vineyards. Francesco

pointed out the different types of grapes. "We use these to make good wines," he said.

Leonardo took his stick and drew a bunch of grapes hanging from one of the vines.

Again, Francesco knelt down and examined the drawing. "Hmm," he said. "I think these grapes are ripe enough to eat." He pretended to pick one up and put it in his mouth. "Yes, yes, quite good," he said.

Once again, Leonardo laughed. He loved his uncle.

Francesco and Leonardo had reached the end of the family's estate, but neither one of them was ready to return to the villa.

"Let's walk toward the mountains, Leonardo," Francesco suggested. "I'll show you the wildflowers and some of the plants my mother uses for medicine. We might also see some rabbits and goats along the way."

Leonardo remembered the goats that his mother milked and the rabbits running in the fields beyond her house, but he had never been close enough to touch them.

The road Francesco and Leonardo were on now was narrow and winding and lined with flowers of all colors. From time to time, Francesco would stop and call a flower by name. Leonardo would repeat it slowly, then, with his finger, he would trace the outline of the flower in the air.

As they made their way along the road, it became narrower and narrower and more rock-strewn until it finally turned into a mountain trail.

"Where are the rabbits?" Leonardo asked. "Where are the goats?"

Francesco looked at the darkening clouds and said, "I think they must be safe in their houses, Leonardo." He pointed to the sky, and Leonardo looked up. "That's where we should be, too, because a storm is approaching."

Suddenly, a bolt of lightning struck a tree just beyond them, causing the trunk to split.

"Let's go see what happened to it," Leonardo suggested.

"No, no, Leonardo, we need to hurry

home," Francesco said. "But when we get there, we'll stand at a window and I'll tell you all about storms."

Leonardo jumped onto Francesco's back, and they headed back to the villa. Leonardo hugged his uncle tightly. He felt safe with him. "You know everything," Leonardo whispered in Francesco's ear. "I want to know everything too."

Francesco laughed. "One day, Leonardo," he said, "I'm sure you will."

CHAPTER TWO
A HAPPY LIFE IN VINCI

By Leonardo's fifth birthday, in 1457, his father, Ser Piero, had married and was living in Florence, a very important city thirty kilometers from Vinci. As a notary, Ser Piero was very busy, and he came home to the village only on feast days and on summer holidays to escape the heat of the city.

Leonardo's mother, Caterina, had also married a man called Accattabriga. She had moved to Campo Zeppi, which Leonardo could walk to in less than half an hour. He no longer saw her at Mass, because she and her new husband attended the church in San Pantaleone. But when they needed to buy food, they had to come to Vinci. At times, Caterina would come to Leonardo's house to see him, but she never wanted to go inside, so they would visit with each other for a few minutes by the side of the road.

Soon, though, Caterina began to have other children, and her visits to Leonardo became less frequent. For a time, Leonardo still walked to Campo Zeppi and although he was welcome and never heard an unkind word from il signore Accattabriga, he began to realize that his mother was so busy with her new family that she had less and less time for him.

When his uncle Francesco gave him a pony, Leonardo began riding it past the Accattabrigases' house, thinking that it would attract their attention, but Leonardo often received only a slight wave of the hand from his mother, so eventually he stopped going. It occurred to Leonardo shortly afterward that nobody seemed to notice that he no longer made the trip.

One day, in 1459, when Leonardo was seven years old, his uncle Francesco said, "I talked to

Father Enzo today, Leonardo, and I asked him to teach you how to read and write."

Leonardo gave Francesco a puzzled look. He liked Father Enzo. In many ways, he reminded Leonardo of Ser Piero. But Leonardo was perfectly happy being with his uncle all day and learning from him.

"He can teach you things that I can't, Leonardo—like how to read and write, which I don't do well," Francesco said, seemingly having understood Leonardo's puzzlement. "And, with Father not being able to do much of the farmwork, I have less time to walk with you around Vinci."

Leonardo knew that his uncle spoke the truth. He had been very busy lately because on many days Leonardo's grandfather never got out of bed.

Leonardo knew how much his uncle missed and needed his grandfather's help, and he had often overheard his grandfather talking to his grandmother about Francesco. They thought Francesco spent too much time daydreaming and not enough time doing things that needed to be done on the farm.

"Then from Father Enzo I will learn to read and write," Leonardo said, "and each day, I will teach you what he has taught me."

That next Sunday, after early Mass, Father Enzo pulled Leonardo aside and said, "I'll see you Monday morning bright and early. I'm going to teach you how to count on the abacus."

Leonardo blinked. He had never heard of an abacus before, but he was intrigued by the word and decided that it was something he wanted to know more about.

Later that day, Leonardo asked his grandfather what an abacus was.

"It's a wooden frame with several rods. The rods have wooden beads on them," Antonio said. "You move the beads back and forth to solve math problems."

"Marco Polo brought one back from China," Francesco added. "I've told you stories about him, Leonardo."

Leonardo remembered. He was one of the

most famous Italians who had ever lived. With his father and uncle, Marco Polo had traveled all across Europe and into Asia, as far as China, following what was called the "Silk Road."

"He brought back lots of things that we Italians had never seen before, like the abacus, and he also showed us how to make ice cream, just like he ate on his trip," Francesco said. He grinned at Leonardo. "You know how much you like ice cream, Nephew. Well, you have Marco Polo to thank for that."

When Monday morning came, Leonardo was up before anyone else, including the servants. While he waited for breakfast, he sat at a table that looked out onto the garden and drew pictures in his notebook. Before, he had crowded his drawings together, so as not to waste the precious paper his father had brought him from Florence. Now, in anticipation of being able to label what he had drawn, he began to leave some space in between each sketch.

"You will soon have a name," he said to the plants and animals in his notebook.

Leonardo knew his drawings weren't alive, but they seemed so lifelike that it was sometimes hard to forget. His grandparents and his uncle agreed. They were constantly amazed at how real Leonardo's drawings looked.

"You are an amazing child, my Leonardo," Antonio would say to him often. "You are simply amazing."

It never occurred to Leonardo to think anything more about these compliments other than to appreciate them and to strive to learn even more about the world around him.

After breakfast, Leonardo walked to the church. Father Enzo was waiting for him in his study, a small room at the rear of the sanctuary. Leonardo had never been there before, and what he saw inside it left him almost speechless. Sunlight from two small windows flooded the room, giving it a warm glow and illuminating the walls, which were lined with shelves full of books. Leonardo knew that this was a place where he could easily spend the rest of his life.

Father Enzo had put a small table and chair next to his larger table. "This is where you will study, Leonardo," he said. "That way, when you have questions, I will be here to answer them."

Leonardo thought it was a wonderful arrangement.

Within days, after Father Enzo had shown Leonardo the acabus, Leonardo was doing difficult math problems.

"Amazing," Father Enzo said. "Simply amazing."

Leonardo was pleased that Father Enzo thought he was doing well, but he decided not to tell him how easy it all was. If he gave Father Enzo the impression that learning was easy and that he could do a lot of it on his own, then Leonardo probably wouldn't be coming to Father Enzo's study, and this was now one of the highlights of his day.

One day, Father Enzo took a book down from the shelf and said, "*Il Milione—'The Travels of Marco Polo.'*" He put his finger on the first word, pronounced it, and then had Leonardo repeat it. Father Enzo continued this process with the next word and the next, until Leonardo was beginning to pronounce the words before Father Enzo could say them.

"Amazing," Father Enzo said.

Soon, Leonardo was reading on his own, with only a few interruptions to ask Father Enzo to help him pronounce and understand a new word.

"When you read, you get inside the head of the person who wrote what you're reading, don't you, Father Enzo?" Leonardo said.

"That is it exactly, Leonardo," Father Enzo said.

"When I'm reading about Marco Polo's travels to China," Leonardo added, "I feel as though I'm traveling with him."

"You have discovered the true joy of knowing how to read, Leonardo," Father Enzo said. "From this day on, your life will never be the same."

After seeing what words on a page could tell

him, Leonardo decided that he now wanted to write some of those words himself. So Father Enzo showed Leonardo how to form his letters.

To Leonardo, it was like drawing, and he took pride in perfectly forming each letter of the alphabet. Soon, Leonardo was able not only to write the names of the plants and animals that he had drawn in his notebooks but to add longer descriptions of them as he wandered the countryside around Vinci, studying nature.

"Amazing," Father Enzo said when Leonardo showed him his latest sketches.

"Thank you," Leonardo said.

Leonardo appreciated hearing these kind remarks from Father Enzo, even if it was always the same word, but in a way he was also disappointed. Leonardo had hoped to find in the priest someone with whom he could have serious discussions about ideas that were coming to him about how the world worked. But Father Enzo now seemed almost too much in awe of him to do this. Leonardo was disappointed that their relationship had changed.

For the next three years, Leonardo sat beside Father Enzo, mastering every subject that the priest presented to him. Often, when the windows were open, Leonardo would hear the other boys of the village playing their games, but never once did he wish that he were among them. Leonardo was where he wanted to be, doing what he wanted to do.

One day, when Leonardo was twelve, he went to Father Enzo's study expecting to spend the day reading and writing, but the priest sighed and said, "I've taught you everything I know, Leonardo. I cannot teach you anymore."

Leonardo had hoped that Father Enzo would still allow him to sit in the study and read books, even though Leonardo had already read most of them twice. But Father Enzo didn't ask him to stay. Disappointed, yet thankful for what he had received from the priest, Leonardo shook Father Enzo's hand and left the church. At first, Leonardo felt lonely, but he soon filled his days by exploring the rocky crevices of the hills around Vinci.

Over the next two years, he discovered plants and animals that no one else seemed to know about. He drew them in his notebooks and labeled them with names he thought fit.

Sometimes, Leonardo would climb along the banks of the Arno River. When he reached a perfect spot, he would lie on his stomach and watch the water flow over the rocks in the riverbed. When he saw what he considered an unusual color arrangement within the stones, he would pull the rock out, sketch the pattern, and then replace the stone in exactly the same spot where he had found it.

One evening, as Leonardo neared his house after having spent most of the day wandering the hills, he noticed a young woman standing on a balcony. Leonardo had never seen her before. Suddenly, his uncle Francesco appeared behind her. The young woman smiled at Francesco, who said something to her, then she kissed his cheek quickly and disappeared into the house.

Leonardo stood for a moment, looking up at the balcony, waiting for his uncle to see him, but Francesco touched the cheek that the young woman had kissed, smiled, then turned and went back into the house himself.

At that moment, Leonardo felt a sadness he didn't understand, but he knew that his life was about to change again.

When Leonardo entered the house, Francesco saw him, brightened, and said, "Come here, Nephew, I want to introduce you to someone."

The young girl Leonardo had seen on the balcony was now standing with his grandmother in the music room.

"Leonardo, this is Maria," Francesco said. "We will be married soon, and she will be your aunt."

Leonardo produced his notebook. "I want to show you something," he said proudly. He opened his notebook to the last two pages. "I found these in a cave today," he said, showing Maria the sketches of some animal bones he had made. "Isn't it marvelous how they're all connected to one another? When you look at these skeletons, you can tell a lot about how our bodies work."

"Oh, my goodness, Leonardo, you are a wonderful artist, but this is such a distasteful subject," Maria said. She handed the notebook back with a shudder. "I wish you would draw pictures of animals that are alive," she added with a smile.

When his uncle gave Maria a smile but said nothing about Leonardo's sketches, Leonardo knew that the relationship had changed forever. Leonardo would no longer be the focus of his attention. Even though Maria and Francesco listened politely as Leonardo finished telling them about that day's adventures in the hills around Vinci, when he finished, they went back to talking about the changes they wanted to make to the villa.

Leonardo went up to his room, hoping to find solace there, but now even this refuge seemed unwelcoming.

Within days, his grandfather Antonio died, leaving Leonardo feeling even more lonely.

After his grandfather's funeral, Leonardo saddled up his horse and rode furiously down the road to his mother's house, but when he got there, no one was around. A neighbor who was walking by told them that they had gone to Siena to see some of Leonardo's stepfather's relatives. The neighbor had no idea when they would return.

Sadly, Leonardo rode back to his house. His father met him at the stables.

"I've been talking to your grandmother and your uncle," Ser Piero told him. "You're fourteen years old now, Leonardo, and we've decided that it's time for you to move to Florence so you can learn to earn your keep."

CHAPTER THREE

THE MAGNIFICENT CITY OF FLORENCE

Leonardo's father had to return to Florence before Leonardo was ready to leave, so on June 15, 1466, he began the trip alone.

Since Florence was less than a day away, even on foot, Leonardo found himself at times lingering along the way. He knew he was excited about living in such an important city as Florence, but a part of him did not want to leave the country. Often, Leonardo would stop to look at the shape of some solitary cloud as it drifted lazily above him in the otherwise cornflower blue sky.

When Leonardo spotted a patch of brilliant red in a green pasture, he left the dusty road and made his way toward it. What he found was a patch of flowers he had never seen before.

Leonardo took his notebook out of his knapsack and began sketching them. When he was finally satisfied that he had captured the flower on paper, he closed his notebook and returned to the road to resume his journey.

Finally, in the late afternoon, Leonardo topped a small hill and saw before him the high walls that encircled the magnificent city of Florence. The great dome of the cathedral rose majestically above the red tile roofs of the surrounding buildings.

Leonardo suddenly experienced something he had never expected. He felt as if he was finally coming home, after having been away for many years. He wasn't quite sure he really understood what was happening, but there was nothing at all unpleasant about the sensations he was now feeling.

Leonardo picked up his pace and soon reached the city gate. As he started through it, someone shouted, "You there! Stop!"

Leonardo turned and saw two guards looking at him.

"What do you want?" Leonardo asked them.

"You may not enter Florence until your belongings have been searched," one of the guards said.

Leonardo walked up to him. "I'm sorry," he said. "I did not know that."

When the guard finished inspecting Leonardo's meager belongings, he asked, "Where are you from?"

"Vinci," Leonardo answered.

"Why are you coming to Florence?" the second guard asked.

"I'm going to live with my father, Ser Piero," Leonardo replied. "He's a notary."

Leonardo immediately noticed a change in the men's attitude toward him.

"We know of him. He's a very important man in Florence," the first guard said. For the first time, he smiled. "With a father such as Ser Piero, you will go far, young man."

Leonardo returned the man's smile, although inside, he didn't feel quite as optimistic. He knew that since his father and mother had never married, there were some careers that the law would not allow him to pursue. If Leonardo thought about that too much, it made him sad, so he tried not to dwell on it. He knew what things he enjoyed doing. He only hoped that they could somehow help him earn a living.

Once inside the gate, Leonardo stopped for a moment to stare at the scenes around him. From their clothes, Leonardo could tell that people from many different lands came to Florence. Leonardo closed his eyes and took a deep breath, filling his nostrils with aromas he had never smelled before.

With his heart pounding from excitement, Leonardo started down the narrow street. At first, after the quiet of the Tuscan countryside, the noises offended his ears, but he was soon able to separate the sounds and turn them into intelligible words and phrases. They came mostly from the street vendors who were hawking their wares.

Leonardo made his way through the crowd toward one of their tables. He pointed to a basket full of dried sticks that were dark brown in color. "What is this?" he asked the vendor. "I've never seen it before."

The vendor regarded Leonardo from head to toe, then grinned. "Spices from India," he said. "You won't find them in the country, young man. You'll only find them in great cities like Florence."

As Leonardo moved past other tables, he saw beautifully dyed cloth, all kinds of things made from leather, and mounds of silk. Still other tables were piled high with fruits and vegetables and meats and cheeses.

The vendor had been right. Leonardo had never seen anything like this in Vinci.

As the sun began to set, Leonardo quickened his pace, not wanting to have to look for his father's house after dark.

He began walking down the center of the street, away from the crowds still looking for things to buy from the vendors, but unfortunately in the path of several heavy carts pulled by donkeys. He had almost been run down by two of those carts when he finally saw on the side of a building the name of the street he had been looking for: Via Larga. This was the street his father lived on.

Leonardo was just about to pass by a doorway of a large stone building on the Via Larga when a priest and a man in a velvet cloak came out in front of him, forcing him to duck out of their way.

"You're lucky, my young friend," a voice from behind him said. "You don't want to anger the Pazzis."

Leonardo looked at the man uncomprehendingly. "I'm not from here, I'm from Vinci. I don't know that name," he said. "I've come to live with my father, Ser Piero."

"I've never heard of him, but I do recognize a Pazzi when I see one," the man said. "They're enemies of the Medicis, and any enemy of the

Medicis is an enemy of mine." The man's dark eyes bore into Leonardo. "I guess you've never heard of the Medicis, either."

"Yes, my uncle told me about the Medicis," Leonardo said. "He said they were the powerful rulers of Florence."

"Your uncle speaks the truth," the man said. He gave Leonardo a smile that sent chills through him. "There are many of us in Florence who want to make sure that it stays that way."

Before Leonardo could say anything else, the man turned and hurried away, quickly disappearing into a throng of people. Leonardo realized that he had been holding his breath. He hoped he never met that man again.

He continued on down the Via Larga in the direction of Ser Piero's house. The man he had just met in the street was not like any of the people he knew in Vinci or in the other towns around his village. The encounter had somewhat unnerved him. Now, he wanted to get to his father's house as soon as possible.

Leonardo tried to recall what his uncle Francesco had told him about Florence and the Medicis. Florence was an independent city-state. It had its own government, its own army, and even its own money. It was ruled by the powerful Medici family, who did not tolerate people who were against them. But the Medicis had actually made Florence the great city it was, because of their love of art. The Medicis had successfully encouraged architects, poets, scientists, painters, philosophers, and sculptors to make their home in Florence. Because of this, Francesco had told Leonardo, Florence was Italy's most exciting and beautiful city.

Leonardo was still caught up in trying to remember every detail of what his uncle had told him about Florence, when he came upon one of the largest buildings he had ever seen in his life. He suddenly remembered that his uncle Francesco had said that before he got to his father's house he would pass the Palazzo Medici, the palace from which Lorenzo de'

Medici ruled Florence. In the courtyard, Leonardo saw a coat of arms and knew it belonged to the Medicis. He felt drawn to the building, wanting to study it in detail, perhaps even to make sketches in his notebooks, but it was now getting to be quite dark, and he knew that he shouldn't tarry.

Finally, Leonardo arrived at his father's house. After identifying himself to a servant, he was let inside.

"You're late," the man said. "You were expected for dinner."

"I'm sorry," Leonardo said. "I was—"

"It is no matter," the servant said, interrupting him. "As dinner is being served now, I have orders to feed you in the kitchen."

Ser Piero's house, although not as large as the house in Vinci, had more magnificent furnishings, and Leonardo felt pride that his father indeed was a successful resident of Florence. He knew now why the guards at the city gate had heard of him.

Leonardo had eaten the last of his bread

and cheese while he was still on the road to Florence, but he hadn't realized until now how hungry he really was. He had no idea what was in the bowl in front of him, but it was the most delicious food he had ever tasted. The flavors seemed to dance on his tongue.

Leonardo had just buttered a second piece of bread when his father entered the kitchen. Leonardo stood up and held out his hand, but instead of shaking it, Ser Piero gave him a hug.

"We thought you'd be here earlier, Leonardo," Ser Piero said, releasing him. "I was beginning to get worried about you."

"It is my fault, Father," Leonardo confessed. "I'm afraid that I was overwhelmed by everything Florence has to offer. I have never seen anything like this before."

Ser Piero smiled. "I wouldn't want to live anywhere else, Leonardo," he said. "Florence has everything that a person needs in life."

"I believe that too," Leonardo said.

"Well, now, we need to talk," Ser Piero said. He took Leonardo's arm. "But first I want you to meet my new wife, Francesca di Ser Giuliano Lanfredini, and then we'll go to my study."

Leonardo's new stepmother gave him a pleasant greeting, wished him luck in his new life in Florence, and then turned her attention back to one of the servants, who seemed very agitated about something. Although she didn't seem as friendly as his father's other wife, Leonardo believed that he would have no trouble getting along with her and fitting right in with the family. He would make it work, he decided.

His father had other plans for him, though.

"Oh, no, Leonardo, you won't be living here," Ser Piero said, when Leonardo said as much. "You're old enough that you need to learn a trade, and that means you'll be staying with the tradesman's family."

Leonardo was disappointed, but he made sure that it didn't show on his face. "Yes, Father," he said.

Ser Piero thought for a minute. "The problem is, what are you really good at?" he said finally. "You've had no formal education. There are a lot of guilds who won't accept you because your mother and I never married."

Leonardo bowed his head.

"What are you *really* good at, Leonardo?" Ser Piero repeated.

"I can draw," Leonardo said, not raising his head.

For several moments, Ser Piero was silent. Then he said, "Leonardo, look at me."

Leonardo raised his head and looked at his father. "I brought some of my sketches with me, if you'd like to see them," he said.

Ser Piero nodded. "Yes, I'd like very much to see them," he said.

Leonardo opened his knapsack and took out one of his notebooks. He handed it to his father.

Ser Piero silently turned the pages.

"As you can see, Father, I like to draw pictures of everything," Leonardo said. "And I want my people and animals and plants to look as real as possible."

Still, Ser Piero said nothing.

Finally, he reached the last page and closed the notebook.

Leonardo held his breath.

"These sketches were done by a true artist, my son," Ser Piero said. He stood up. "Tomorrow, you and I shall go to the *bottega* of Andrea del Verrocchio. He's one of the most important artists in Florence. I'm going to ask him to take you on as one of his apprentices."

CHAPTER FOUR
VERROCCHIO'S
BOTTEGA

That night, Leonardo slept in a servant's room just off the kitchen, but it was only because some of his stepmother's relatives had come to Florence unexpectedly and were occupying the other bedrooms. Leonardo didn't mind. The bed was comfortable and, besides, he knew he was too excited about what the next day would bring to sleep very much. Still, the next morning, his father had to shake his shoulder several times to awaken him.

"Lucia has breakfast ready for you, Leonardo," Ser Piero said, "but you must hurry, as I want to talk to Verrocchio as soon as his *bottega* opens. I need be at the Palazzo Medici before ten."

"Yes, Father," Leonardo said. He sat up and rubbed his eyes. As Ser Piero started out of the room, Leonardo added, "Thank you for everything, Father. I will not disappoint you."

Leonardo climbed out of bed and splashed his face with the cold water that was in a pitcher on a small table next to the door.

His clothes were still dusty from his journey to Florence the day before, so he brushed them off as best as he could. He hoped that the great Verrocchio would be more interested in his drawings than in how he looked.

When Leonardo was dressed, he stepped into the kitchen and received a smile from a woman he assumed was Lucia.

"Ah, Leonardo!" Lucia said. "I hope you're hungry."

Leonardo nodded.

"Your father tells me you are a great artist," Lucia said as she set a plate of cheese, sausage, and bread in front of him. "Well, if you are half as great as Ser Piero says you are, you will go far in Florence, because the Medicis appreciate artists." She sighed. "I wish my sons were artists, but they spend their days taking care of the Medici horses, which mostly means cleaning up their manure."

"That is an honorable occupation too, Lucia," Leonardo said. "The most important thing to know is if they're happy."

"Oh, they are happy, Leonardo, they are," Lucia said. "They also get to exercise the horses, and that's when they pretend they are important members of Florentine society."

Leonardo smiled. "They do sound happy, truly," he said.

"Leonardo?"

Leonardo turned. His father was standing at the door to the kitchen, dressed for the day. Leonardo quickly put the last piece of bread in his mouth, thanked Lucia, and grabbed his knapsack.

"I wish you good fortune," Lucia called after him.

"Thank you," Leonardo shouted back.

Outside, the street in front of Ser Piero's

house was full of people going in both directions. As they walked along, Ser Piero pointed out the various buildings and told Leonardo what went on inside of them. Leonardo was amazed that his father seemed to know everything that was happening in Florence.

When they reached the Via dell' Agnolo, Ser Piero said, "Verrocchio's *bottega* is on this street, Leonardo. We aren't too far from it now."

"Are the streets in Florence always this crowded with people?" Leonardo asked.

"Always, Leonardo," Ser Piero said.

Leonardo's uncle Francesco had told him that Florence was started as a Roman colony in 59 B.C. In the sixth century, it was captured by the Lombards, a Germanic tribe, who controlled it for several hundred years, until it emerged as an important city-state under the Medicis, a powerful banking family.

Finally, Leonardo and his father arrived at Andrea del Verrocchio's studio. One of the apprentices was just opening the front door.

Suddenly, a chicken darted from between Leonardo's legs and disappeared inside the *bottega*.

Leonardo expected the apprentice to run after the chicken and chase it out, but the apprentice only smiled and said, "That's Pia. I think she's angry that she had to wait on me to open the door this morning. She wasn't in by ten o'clock, so she had to stay out all night. I'm surprised she didn't end up in someone's pot for dinner." He smiled again. "Are you the new *apprendista*?" he asked, using the Italian word for "apprentice."

"That's what we are here to talk to Verrocchio about," Ser Piero said. "Would you take us to him?"

"Gladly," the apprentice said. "My name's Pandolfo."

"I'm Leonardo," Leonardo said.

As he stepped inside Verrocchio's studio, Leonardo's eyes opened wide in amazement. If he had been asked to describe the most wonderful place to be—outside of heaven, of course, as he crossed himself—it would be here.

The *bottega* was almost as busy as one of Florence's streets. It was a beehive of activity.

"There's Verrocchio," Pandolfo said. "He is the one in the middle of the room, waving his arms around in the air, telling everyone what to do and where to go."

Leonardo looked at the man who was not only the official sculptor of the Medici family but was considered the greatest sculptor of his time. He had dark, curly hair and a square face. He also had a stern look, which Leonardo thought made him seem unfriendly. He wasn't sure that was a good sign.

"Leonardo, you stay here with Pandolfo," Ser Piero said. "I need to talk to Verrocchio alone for a few minutes."

"All right, Father," Leonardo said.

Leonardo looked around the *bottega*. Paintbrushes, mallets, and chisels almost covered the walls of the shop. What space was left was taken up by sketches showing projects in various stages of completion.

Just then, a pig ran squealing into the

bottega. It was soon followed by two laughing children, who chased it around the shop until they finally managed to get it to the front door of the shop, where it ran back out into the street.

What amazed Leonardo more than what he had just seen was that nobody seemed to notice. The activity in the shop didn't stop just because cackling chickens, squealing pigs, and laughing children were running around and through and under things.

At the rear of the *bottega* an apprentice was firing up a kiln. To Leonardo's right, two more apprentices were hammering armor. Behind them, on a long table, another apprentice was pounding stone.

"Why is he doing that?" Leonardo asked Pandolfo.

"He's turning the stone into powder," Pandolfo replied. "We add it to different materials to make them smoother and stronger."

"I had no idea that Verrocchio did so many different things in his shop," Leonardo said. "I thought he was just a sculptor and a painter."

Pandolfo shook his head. "The *bottega* receives orders not only for paintings and for sculptures but for various decorations for the great houses: armor, jewelry, and many, many other things—whatever the people of Florence want," he said. "It's all art, Leonardo."

"You're right," Leonardo agreed.

"Don't worry about it, though," Pandolfo said. "You won't have to learn everything at once."

"Verrocchio has to agree to take me on as an apprentice first," Leonardo said. "He may not—"

"Leonardo!"

Ser Piero was calling him.

Leonardo turned to Pandolfo. "Will you come with me?" he asked.

Pandolfo shook his head. "No, I need to get to my table or Verrocchio will scold me, but afterward, I'll show you around."

"I hope there will be an 'afterward,'" Leonardo said.

"There will be," Pandolfo said. He patted Leonardo's shoulder. "I can tell by your eyes that you are an artist."

Leonardo accepted the compliment without saying anything, and hurried over to where his father and Verrocchio were waiting for him.

"Master Verrocchio has agreed to look at your drawings, Leonardo," Ser Piero said.

"Thank you, sir," Leonardo said. He took his notebook from the knapsack and handed it to Verrocchio.

Verrocchio began leafing through the pages.

Leonardo watched Verrocchio's face closely for any sign of what he was thinking, but Verrocchio's expression never changed.

Finally, Verrocchio closed the notebook and returned it to Leonardo.

Leonardo's heart sank. His dreams were ending here, he thought. Verrocchio would not take him on as an apprentice because he wasn't good enough. How Leonardo wished he had hated this place when he first saw it instead of falling in love with it and wishing he could live there forever.

"What do you think?" Ser Piero asked.

Leonardo wanted to cry out to his father to remain silent. He didn't want to hear from Verrocchio that he wasn't worthy of remaining in his *bottega* one more moment than was necessary.

"I have never seen such talent in someone so young," Verrocchio said. He turned to Leonardo. "It will be an honor to have you here."

Suddenly, Leonardo's heart began to pound. There was such a ringing in his ears that he wasn't quite sure he had heard Verrocchio correctly.

"Ripeta, per piacere, maestro," Leonardo managed to say.

Verrocchio laughed. "I said that I want very much for you to be an apprentice in my *bottega*, Leonardo!"

CHAPTER FIVE
THE APPRENTICE

Leonardo shook hands with Ser Piero and said, "Thank you again, Father. I know I'm going to be very happy here."

"I certainly want that for you, Leonardo," Ser Piero said, "but you must also be productive."

"Oh, I have no doubt that Leonardo will soon know more than I know," Verrocchio said with a big grin. "I plan to keep my eye on this son of yours, Ser Piero. He's going to go far."

Ser Piero left the *bottega* without a backward glance, but Leonardo understood that his father was a very busy man and needed to be at the Palazzo Medici shortly.

"Pandolfo! Take Leonardo upstairs and show him where he'll be sleeping. He can also leave his knapsack there," Verrocchio said. "Don't tarry, either, as I have things for both of you boys to do."

"Come on, Leonardo," Pandolfo said. "There's an empty bed in my room."

Leonardo followed Pandolfo to the wooden steps that led to the second floor of the *bottega*. Halfway up, Leonardo stopped for a moment to survey the scene below him. He could hardly believe that he had finally discovered a world where he felt he really belonged.

"I knew Verrocchio would take you on as an apprentice," Pandolfo said as he led Leonardo down a dim corridor. "I'm a very good judge of people."

"I'm glad you believed in me, Pandolfo," Leonardo said. He grinned. "I'll try to live up to your expectations."

Leonardo looked around the small room. It was cramped, but there was a pleasant feel to it. Leonardo knew that besides being a place to sleep, it would also be somewhere he and Pandolfo and the other apprentices could discuss their art with one another. Leonardo was looking forward to that.

When Leonardo and Pandolfo went back downstairs, Verrocchio said, "Leonardo, the newest apprentice always sweeps the floors. It's a very important job. The inside of the *bottega* must never offend our patrons."

Pandolfo handed Leonardo a broom. As he worked his way around the *bottega*, Leonardo had a chance to see up close what was going on in the rest of the shop and to meet some of the other apprentices.

Bartolomeo was making some gold jewelry. Uziello was making some silver candlestick holders. Cicanchi was making a small bronze statue of a horse. Giuliamo was making a wooden altarpiece. Domenico was making a clay model of the head of a Medici child that he would later carve from marble.

At the back of the shop, several other apprentices were working on a float that would be used in the marriage celebration of some important people in Florence.

Without realizing it, Leonardo had swept the *bottega* three times before Verrocchio finally came up to him and said, "Leonardo, of all of my apprentices, I have never had one who swept the stones this clean. Honestly, dear boy, once around is enough."

Some of the other apprentices laughed.

Leonardo blushed. He hadn't realized what he had done. "I was watching carefully what everyone was doing, Master Verrocchio," he said. "I want to learn what they know as fast as possible."

Verrocchio took a deep breath and looked up at the ceiling. "What have I agreed to?" he said. When he lowered his head, he was smiling. "Normally, Leonardo, an apprentice is given mundane jobs to do, mainly because they need to be done but also so he can have some time to learn what all we do here. But I'm beginning to think that you will soon be apprenticing the rest of us." He looked around the *bottega*. "I have an idea. I need someone to deliver a necklace to the Principessa Strozzi."

He turned back to Leonardo. "Would you be interested in doing that for me?"

"Yes!" Leonardo said excitedly. "I'll do that."

Verrocchio took a small purple velvet bag from a cabinet and handed it to Leonardo. "The Palazzo Strozzi is, naturally, on the Via degli Strozzi," he said. "Here. I'll show you how to get there." Verrocchio took a small piece of paper and drew a map. He handed it to Leonardo. "Don't tarry. The Principessa Strozzi's maid is expecting this. Her name is Maddalena," he said. "The Principessa Strozzi isn't one to tolerate apprentices who are late, and since she is one of our best clients, I don't want to make her angry."

Leonardo hurriedly left the shop. Two blocks down on the Via Largo, he turned to his right and, glancing at Verrocchio's map from time to time, expertly wove his way through the crowded streets. Soon, Leonardo began to feel as though he had lived in Florence all of his life. Thanks to Verrocchio's expert cartography, Leonardo reached the Palazzo Strozzi in what he thought was very good time.

Leonardo rang a bell and identified himself to the man who opened the door. The man took Leonardo to a small room and told him to wait.

Within minutes, a door on the opposite side of the room opened and a young girl appeared. She smiled at Leonardo.

Leonardo smiled back. "I have the Principessa Strozzi's necklace," he said. "Are you Maddalena?"

The girl nodded.

Leonardo handed her the purple velvet bag.

"I've never seen you before," Maddalena said.

"I'm new. I just started today," Leonardo said. "I want to be a great artist."

"What's your name?" Maddalena asked.

"Leonardo," Leonardo said. He hesitated. "Leonardo da Vinci," he added.

"Well, Leonardo da Vinci," Maddalena

said. "I'll make sure that the *Principessa* Strozzi remembers your name."

Maddalena gave Leonardo another smile and disappeared behind the door.

The young man who had first answered his ring let Leonardo out of the Palazzo Strozzi, and he retraced his route back to Verrocchio's shop.

When he got there, Verrocchio was waiting for him. "Just as I expected," he said. "You completed your first task in the fastest time yet."

Leonardo smiled. "Now what?" he asked.

Verrocchio looked around at the other apprentices, who were all smiling at Leonardo. "Now what?" he asked them.

"I can teach him how to work in gold!" Bartolomeo shouted.

"I can teach him how to work in silver!" Uziello said.

"No, no, not yet. That will come," Verrocchio said. He scratched his chin. "I think Leonardo needs to learn how to prepare canvases, make brushes, grind paints, and mix colors." He looked at Leonardo. "How does that sound?"

"It sounds wonderful," Leonardo told him.

Verrocchio led Leonardo to a small room off the side of the *bottega*. "We are all artists here, Leonardo, and proud of our various talents. But in order to survive, we must first create works that our clients commission us to do. Sometimes you may get angry when what you're asked to make goes against how you would create the piece, but when that happens, you must then hide your feelings and do exactly what you've been paid to do. After that, after you have made enough money so that you can survive, you can then listen to your muses and create works of art in your own style." Verrocchio stopped, turned, and put both hands on Leonardo's shoulders. "Do you understand what I mean? To some people in Florence, we are mere craftsmen, not artists."

Leonardo nodded.

"It doesn't disappoint you?" Verrocchio asked.

Leonardo shook his head.

"I am glad, for I truly believe that you have extraordinary talent, Leonardo," Verrocchio said. "I want to do what I can to give you a place where you can blossom."

For the next several days, working with some of the other apprentices, Leonardo learned how to grind various rocks to make colors, and make some of the finest brushes that Verrocchio had ever seen.

Several times during the day, though, Verrocchio would tell everyone to stop what he was doing, take out his sketch pad, and practice drawing.

"This is wonderful," Leonardo whispered to Pandolfo, "but won't we get behind in our other work?"

"This is part of our training, too, Leonardo," Pandolfo said. "We are here not only to work, we are also here to learn."

That day, Verrocchio had set a clay model of clasped hands on a table and asked all of the apprentices to draw it. While most of the apprentices were struggling, trying to get the hands of the model just right, Leonardo quickly drew what he saw, then turned his attention to Pandolfo's hands. Pandolfo was too busy trying to get the fingers of the model right to notice what Leonardo was doing.

After everyone had finished, Verrocchio went around, looking at what his apprentices had done. When he came to Leonardo, he took one look at his sketches and said, "I'm painting a picture of Saint John baptizing Jesus, and I want you to help me."

Leonardo gasped. "I couldn't do that, sir," he managed to say. "You're the master."

"I may be the master, Leonardo, but I cannot draw as well as you can," Verrocchio admitted. "I'm having trouble with the angels, especially their hands, and what I see in your sketches is exactly what I have been looking for."

For a few seconds, the *bottega* was silent, then all at once, it erupted into applause. Leonardo knew that he had now been accepted as one of them. There was no jealousy. They were all there to work together.

For the next several days, the only thing that Leonardo did was help Verrocchio finish the painting he had been commissioned to do for one of the churches in Florence. Verrocchio showed Leonardo where he wanted the angels in the picture. With great care, Leonardo painted the angels, finished the background, and then showed it to Verrocchio.

"What do you think?" Leonardo asked.

"I think it is much finer than anything else in the picture," Verrocchio said. "I shall never again pick up a paintbrush."

At first Leonardo thought Verrocchio had just been joking with him, but when Verrocchio began concentrating on his sculptures, Leonardo realized he had been telling the truth.

When Leonardo approached him about this, telling him that he was sorry, Verrocchio said, "I am here to train my apprentices, Leonardo. Have you no idea what a thrill it is when you discover that one of your apprentices is better than you are?" He gave Leonardo a hug. "Your skill as an artist is being told all over Florence," he added. "You will soon have no time to worry about me."

Now when Verrocchio made the apprentices stop what they were doing to work on their own art, Leonardo helped him by going around and making suggestions about their sketches. Everyone was happy to hear what Leonardo had to say.

One day, Verrocchio said, "I feel that you are all ready to move on from drawing to painting in a new technique that I am very excited about." He held up a small portrait. "Instead of mixing colors with water, the Flemings mix them with oil and, as you see, it produces something very exciting to look at."

Leonardo in particular was quite interested in the new medium, and when he wasn't making tapestries and carpets, painting banners for festivals, or making the sets and costumes for the many pageants held in Florence each year, he studied every Flemish painting Verrocchio was able to find for him so that he could master this technique. Leonardo had already decided that he now wanted to work with paints mixed with oils.

Leonardo's first year in Florence passed quickly. In addition to everything else he was learning in the *bottega*, he had also resumed his study of mathematics, remembering what Father Enzo had taught him earlier. But now, with Verrocchio's help, he was learning to understand perspective so that he could create the illusion of a painting being three-dimensional. Most of the paintings at the time were flat, but Leonardo thought that there should be a way to make them look more lifelike.

Recalling the bones he had found in the cave near Vinci, Leonardo also wanted to study the anatomy of people and animals so that he could make them seem more real in his paintings.

CHAPTER SIX

LEONARDO, THE MATHEMATICIAN

"Let's go get some ice cream," Pandolfo said one evening when the shop was closed and most of the apprentices had left for a stroll along one of the busy streets.

Leonardo looked up from sketching. "I'll go with you to get some ice cream, Pandolfo, if you'll go with me to get what I want."

"What's that?" Pandolfo asked.

"The bones of dead people," Leonardo replied.

When Leonardo saw the horrified look on Pandolfo's face, he explained why he wanted them.

"I know a physician here in Florence who can help you, Leonardo," Pandolfo said. "I painted a picture of his wife's dog, which made

64

her very happy. He treats me whenever I am ill, and he does not expect me to give him anything in return." Pandolfo pulled Leonardo closer to him. "I have seen dead bodies in his house. This physician dissects a body with a large knife so that he can discover what made the person die, and then, by knowing that, one of his servants whispered to me, keep other people from dying the same way."

For just a moment, Leonardo shuddered within, wondering if his stomach would be turned by such a sight. But the chance to see exactly how a human being was put together underneath his skin would be well worth it, he decided. Leonardo believed that knowing that would make his paintings much more realistic.

At noon, with their morning's work out of the way, and with Verrocchio's blessing, Leonardo and Pandolfo left the *bottega* and headed for the physician's house in the Via dell'Acqua.

When they arrived, a servant, recognizing Pandolfo, opened the door and ushered them into a little waiting room.

Within minutes, the physician appeared. He was wearing a thick leather apron over his clothes.

"Are you feeling ill again, Pandolfo?" the physician asked.

Pandolfo shook his head. "I want to introduce you to Leonardo da Vinci," he said. "He is one of Verrocchio's new apprentices."

"Ah," the physician said. He looked at Leonardo. "Do you want to paint portraits of my wife's dogs too?" he asked.

"No, il dottore," Leonardo replied. "I want to study the skeletons of human beings. I think it will make me a better painter because it will make my subjects seem more lifelike."

For just a minute, the physician's face seemed puzzled, then he looked at Pandolfo.

"I apologize, il dottore," Pandolfo said. "When I was here last, you know, when I was coughing up blood, I made the wrong turn, leaving the room where you examined me, and that's when I saw . . ." Pandolfo stopped. "If I have betrayed you, I am sorry, and we will leave at once."

"Oh, no, no, Pandolfo," the physician said. "It is just an unusual request, that's all." He turned back to Leonardo. "It isn't often that someone wants to do this, Leonardo," he said. "Unfortunately, there are also many physicians who don't want to dissect human beings, even if it means discovering the truth about what diseases do to a body." He paused again. "It isn't an easy task, son. Do you have a strong stomach?"

Leonardo nodded. "I believe I do," he replied. "I will tell my stomach that what I am doing is important to my work."

The physician smiled. "That is exactly what I tell my stomach too," he said. "It usually works."

"When do you want me to come?" Leonardo asked.

"I'm dissecting a young man now," the physician said. "He was brought to me this morning. The parents are devastated by his death. They want me to try to discover why it happened, if I can, so it won't happen to their other sons. You may join me now, if you wish."

"Yes, I would like that very much," Leonardo said. He turned to Pandolfo. "Do you have time?"

"I am going to let you do this by yourself, Leonardo. This is not something I want to know about now," Pandolfo said quickly. "I'll return to the *bottega* and tell Verrocchio. He will not mind if you spend the rest of the afternoon here, I'm sure."

Pandolfo was right. In fact, when Leonardo returned that evening, Verrocchio asked him to tell the rest of the apprentices what he had learned.

Leonardo showed the other apprentices his notebooks. He had made several drawings, which stunned everyone.

"Is that really the way we all look inside, Leonardo?" Domenico asked.

Leonardo nodded. "At first, I couldn't figure

out how to show the different organs in the places where they actually are, because they lie on top of one another, but then I decided to make the ones in front transparent so that when you're looking at them, they're all in the correct location within the body."

"Outstanding work, Leonardo," Verrocchio said. "You are a genius."

Bartolomeo stepped back and studied the rest of the apprentices for several minutes. "It works," he said. "It really works!"

"What really works?" Giuliamo asked.

"If you know what a person looks like on the inside, you have an entirely different perspective of what he looks like on the outside," Bartolomeo explained. He turned to Leonardo. "No one has ever thought about that before, Leonardo. You're the first."

Leonardo's standing among the apprentices, already high, soared even higher. To the young men, he seemed to know as much if not more than Verrocchio. In many circles this would have caused a lot of dissension, but not in Verrocchio's *bottega*. Verrocchio reacted to Leonardo's skills in anatomy in much the same way as he had when Leonardo had painted the angels in the picture of Saint John baptizing Jesus. He felt honored to have among his apprentices someone whom he knew history would not forget.

Over the next few weeks, Leonardo visited the physician often, always with Verrocchio's blessings. When he returned to the *bottega,* he would show Verrocchio and the apprentices his sketches.

When there were no human bodies to dissect, Leonardo and the physician dissected animals. Soon, Leonardo's notebook was full of intricate drawings of monkeys, birds, frogs, bears, and cows.

"Look carefully at this skeleton of a bird, especially the bones in the wings," Leonardo said. After everyone had studied the drawing, Leonardo turned the page. "Now here I've drawn those same bones, which I myself could

70

make out of a lightweight wood, I think, and I have attached them to the arms of a man."

Several of the apprentices gasped.

"What are you saying, Leonardo?" Verrocchio asked.

"I see no reason why man, one day, with wings attached to his arms like the wings of this bird, might not fly," Leonardo said. When no one said anything, Leonardo added, "If you think of the things we have now, right here in Florence, which we didn't have a hundred years ago, are not you astonished?"

"Leonardo is right," Cicanchi said. "We artists are the ones who need to be dreaming of what else man can do one day, and we need to be drawing it on paper or painting it on canvas."

The rest of the apprentices agreed.

"Well, there will be plenty of time later for dreaming, but now we have work to do," Verrocchio said. "I received a very important commission today, which we shall all need to work on together."

"What is it?" Uziello asked excitedly.

"The Church wants us to make a great bronze sphere and cross to be placed on top of Santa Maria del Fiore," Verrocchio said. "It will be twenty feet across, and I have calculated that it will weight close to two tons."

"It is the one that Brunelleschi designed before he died!" Domenico said. "We have been asked to finish what Brunelleschi started?"

Verrocchio nodded. "Yes, that is it exactly," he said.

Now, it was Leonardo's turn to be astonished. It was one thing to open up a man or a cow to look inside and draw what you saw, but it was an almost impossible task to make such a huge sphere and then figure out a way to put it on top of Florence's cathedral—to finish the work started almost two hundred years ago by Arnolfo di Cambio.

Leonardo knew that although Giotto had designed the bell tower of the Santa Maria del Fiore, several other architects and artists had worked on it. It was Filippo Brunnelleschi who had astounded the world when he erected the dome, because it did not have any of the external supports that were usually necessary. Back then, everyone thought what he planned to do was impossible, yet he had done it. Now, the Church was asking for something that, to Leonardo, seemed almost impossible too. But Verrocchio had not declined the commission, because, Leonardo was sure, their master had already figured out in his head exactly how they were going to do it.

Starting the next day, almost all of the other work was put on hold—with the exception of tombstones, which couldn't wait, because the people whose names were carved on them needed to be buried. But when other clients came in, disgruntled because their wives' jewelry was unfinished or the paintings of their children were still in sketches on the canvas, Verrocchio would take them aside and show them the plans for the giant sphere that were now covering almost all of the wall space in the *bottega*.

"Oh, Verrocchio, it will be magnificent," all of the clients said. "You must not worry about such a minor thing as what I have requested."

Soon, word spread about what Verrocchio and his apprentices were doing, so almost no clients came in to ask when their art pieces would be ready.

Working steadily, sometimes very late into the night, Verrocchio and his apprentices cast the metal and assembled the sphere, which now took up most of the floor space of the *bottega*.

When the sphere was finally finished, Verrocchio said, "The easy part is over. We now have to figure out a way to get it to the top of the cupola and attach it to the lantern. From this point on, we pass from art into engineering."

Among Verrocchio and the other apprentices in the *bottega*, Leonardo was the only one who had some training in mathematics, so he was given the task of figuring out how to hoist the sphere to the top of the lantern. He also had to figure out how to secure it once it was there, so that strong winds would not topple it and send it tumbling into the streets of Florence.

Over the next few weeks, Leonardo, remembering his study of science and geometry with Father Enzo, designed a set of cranes and pulleys that he was sure would do the job.

When Leonardo explained to Verrocchio and the other apprentices how it would work, they were all astonished.

"Is there nothing that you cannot do, Leonardo?" Pandolfo asked.

"Oh, yes, my friend, there are still many things," Leonardo replied. "I am only nineteen years old. I have just begun to learn."

On May 27, 1471, all of Florence came to watch the hoisting of the great sphere to the top of the marble lantern of Santa Maria del Fiore.

Leonardo's cranes and pulleys worked perfectly.

CHAPTER SEVEN

ABANDONED PROJECTS

Under Verrocchio's guiding hand, Leonardo continued to grow artistically over the next two years.

"You have the ability to master everything, Leonardo," Verrocchio told him one morning. "You already know what you're good at—better at than I am, in fact—but there's so much more that you can do."

Leonardo agreed. He was not content to be known for just a few artistic achievements; he wanted to do it all—not out of arrogance, everyone knew, but because he truly believed that he had God-given talents that should not be wasted, that should be pushed to their limits.

In addition to what he was already doing, Leonardo started making pieces of furniture for some of Verrocchio's wealthier clients, musical instruments for their children, and surgical tools for the physician with whom he continued to study the anatomy of humans and animals.

When Leonardo wasn't working in the *bottega,* he enjoyed strolling around Florence.

"I doubt if I shall ever see everything this city has to offer," Leonardo told Pandolfo one afternoon as they walked together on the Via del Corso. "Florence is so alive and is constantly changing, just like humans and animals do, as they grow. Each time you visit a street after you've been away for some time, that street no longer resembles the street you remember."

Pandolfo looked up at Leonardo. "Well, some of us change, anyway," he said with a chuckle. "You, my friend, are tall and handsome." He sighed. "I am short, and yes, I will say it, I am *round,* and I have always been that way, and I shall always be that way."

Leonardo laughed. "You eat too much pasta," he said.

"I know, I know," Pandolfo agreed, "but other than my work at the *bottega*, pasta is the only other love of my life." Pandolfo stopped in the middle of the street. "Look at you, Leonardo. You're dressed in the latest fashions. You know how to charm Verrocchio's clients so that we receive twice as many commissions as we would otherwise." Pandolfo threw up his hands and started walking again. "You know how to *talk* to people. I used to know, I think, but now all I do is stutter and stammer. I don't like myself at all, Leonardo."

"Stop it, Pandolfo. You are a master craftsman, a famed sculptor," Leonardo said. "There are clients who will have no other's works but yours."

"You're quite right about that, Leonardo," Pandolfo said. He stopped and grinned at Leonardo. "I just wanted to hear you say it."

Leonardo laughed. "I suspected as much," he said. "Let's cross the street here. I want to show you something."

For the next hour, Leonardo and Pandolfo

wandered around the Piazza del Duomo, studying the shrines, the statues, and the frescoes.

After a while, Pandolfo looked up to see where the sun was, and said, "I think we should go back to the *bottega*, Leonardo. Verrocchio wants us to grind up some pigment and then mix it with linseed oil to see if it will make a better paint than that mixed with walnut oil."

"I'm not ready to go yet, Pandolfo," Leonardo said, not taking his eyes off the fresco in front of him. "I want to—"

"We must go, Leonardo," Pandolfo insisted. "If we don't, then . . . well, Verrocchio will . . ." He hesitated.

Leonardo turned away from the fresco and looked at his friend. "You seem rather anxious about something all of a sudden, Pandolfo," he said. "What will happen if we don't return right away?" he asked.

Pandolfo bowed his head. "I don't like the way some of the apprentices talk about you these days," he said. He looked up at

Leonardo. "We need to go back to the *bottega*."

"What do they say, Pandolfo?" Leonardo asked.

Pandolfo took a deep breath and let it out. "They say you waste a lot of time wandering around Florence. They say you dream too much. They say you start projects, but that you never finish them," he said. "That's what they say, Leonardo, and . . . well, they're right."

Leonardo shrugged. "I don't think that wandering around Florence and studying the magnificent art of this city is a waste of time. And artists *have* to be dreamers to think up their creations," he said. "As for not finishing projects, well, yes, I know that I have done that before, but I'll finish them all one of these days." Leonardo sighed. "Sometimes, Pandolfo, when I'm in the middle of one of my commissions, I start thinking about other things I want to do, so I stop and work on those projects," he said. "You can't always rush art, Pandolfo. You sometimes have to stand back and let it grow for a while of its own accord."

"I understand that, Leonardo. I understand *you*, I think, because we're friends. And friends trust friends, and they tolerate their behavior," Pandolfo said. "But the people who commission you to paint their portraits are only interested in seeing themselves hanging in their great halls as soon as possible."

For several minutes, Leonardo walked in silence beside Pandolfo as they headed back to the *bottega*. Finally, as they started through the *piazza*, he said, "I get bored, I guess, Pandolfo. I really enjoy the first part of painting, but then . . . I don't know what happens to me. I . . . I don't want to talk about it now."

Leonardo knew that Pandolfo, being the friend that he was, wouldn't press him to explain further. Instead, the two of them walked in a companionable silence.

It gave Leonardo time to reflect on what Pandolfo had said. Actually, he had only put into words what Leonardo already knew but didn't want to face.

When he was commissioned to do a painting, whether for an individual client or for a church, he thoroughly enjoyed sketching out and planning the composition of the picture. In fact, it was not unusual for him to linger over this stage for months. The next step, the cartoon, Leonardo also enjoyed. Here, he created the finished sketch from which the actual painting would be made. The cartoon sketch was the same size as the actual subject of the painting. Often that meant Leonardo would have to glue several sheets of paper together to create a space large enough to hold his design. When this was finished, Leonardo attached the sheets either to a wooden panel or to a canvas. After that, following the outline of the sketch, Leonardo punched little holes in the paper. For the next step, he pressed black chalk through the holes and, when he removed the paper, the picture had been transferred onto the surface underneath, and Leonardo was now ready to paint.

What followed next was called the underpainting, and this was where, Leonardo admitted to himself, he would start to lose interest. He only wished he knew *why*. Using brown and gray paint, Leonardo painted the shadows that gave the picture its three-dimensionality. When the underpainting was finished, Leonardo put in the color, which meant adding several layers of oil paint.

"Do people really talk about how I simply abandon my projects, Pandolfo?" Leonardo asked suddenly.

"Yes, Leonardo, they do," Pandolfo said softly.

Leonardo knew that something had started happening to him recently, when he reached the underpainting stage. For some reason, which he didn't yet understand, he would simply shut down. He couldn't face finishing the project. It would begin to suffocate him. In fact, he vividly remembered the first time it had happened. He had found it difficult to breathe, and he knew he had to escape, to do something else. Once again, as he often did, he left the *bottega* and wandered the streets of

Florence, watching the wealthy citizens as they came and went, wondering what it would be like to have enough money to do what they were doing. Sometimes it would take Leonardo hours before he could even think about returning to the *bottega* if he had to resume the task he had abandoned, so it soon became easier and easier for him simply to ignore what he had been working on and start something new. Verrocchio had tolerated this, refusing to scold Leonardo, because, as Leonardo had overheard him say many times, this was how one dealt with geniuses. Of course, it had helped that some of the apprentices often worked on the same projects together, but now they had begun to feel that they weren't really working together with Leonardo on his projects as much as they were cleaning up after him.

When Leonardo and Pandolfo finally arrived back at the *bottega*, all of the apprentices were at the back of the shop, with Verrocchio holding forth on some different techniques of oil painting that were just now reaching Florence and the rest of Italy with the visits from artists from other parts of the European continent.

Pandolfo quickly took his place among the rest of the apprentices, but Leonardo hung back, and neither Verrocchio nor anyone else said anything. With one ear, Leonardo would listen to what Verrocchio was saying—just in case his master had acquired some new knowledge from one of the visiting artists—but with the other ear, he would listen to himself in case his heart tried to tell him what caused him to behave the way he did. At times, Leonardo thought he had everything he could possibly wish for; yet at other times, he believed he had nothing compared to what he thought he ought to have. It was almost impossible to explain to anyone what he meant.

Finally, Verrocchio's lecture was over. When the apprentices went to their tables to practice what he had been talking about, Verrocchio wandered over to where Leonardo was standing.

Putting his arm around Leonardo's shoulders, Verrocchio said, "I wish there was something I could say, Leonardo, to help you see more clearly what it is you want to do with your life, but I am without words."

Leonardo turned his head away. "I am without words too," he whispered.

CHAPTER EIGHT

THE JOKESTER

One of the things that Leonardo liked most about Verrocchio's *bottega* was that, from time to time, other artists in Florence would drop by to ask Verrocchio how he would approach the creation of a certain work of art.

Even with all of the praise that Verrocchio heaped on him, Leonardo still considered Verrocchio to be his master, and marveled at his fount of knowledge. Just when Leonardo thought that Verrocchio couldn't possibly know anything else about art, Verrocchio surprised everyone with his new ideas.

When the visiting artists were there, Verrochio's apprentices would often stop what they were doing so they could listen in. But sometimes, this was also an opportunity to visit with some of the apprentices who accompanied their masters.

With Uziello playing the flute in the corner, all of the apprentices—Leonardo among them—would argue about which *bottega* produced the best art and whose ideas were the most likely to impress the Medicis. After the arguments were over, though, they would spend the rest of the time teaching one another their different techniques.

"Everything in the world is connected in some way, and I want to learn about everything," Leonardo told the other apprentices.

But when Leonardo started to explain what he did when he and the physician were dissecting human bodies, some of the apprentices said, "Oh, Leonardo! Could we talk about something more pleasant?"

"Of course," Leonardo said. "Let me tell you how I paint angels."

For the next hour, Leonardo detailed how, by studying the wings of birds, he was able to paint the wings of angels so realistically. To the delight of the visiting apprentices, he took out his notebook, sketched the skeletal outline of a bird's wing, added the feathers, then attached them to the body of an angel. While the apprentices attempted to do the same thing, Leonardo walked among them, pointing out what was right and what was wrong.

As the apprentices were leaving, one of them said, "When we come next time, I want you to show us how you draw horses, Leonardo."

"I shall do that," Leonardo promised them. "I'm going to the Medici stables tomorrow, and I'll have some new sketches for you to look at."

Almost everyone in Florence knew that Leonardo loved horses. He spent hours watching the way they moved and sketching them in minute detail.

The next day, Leonardo hurriedly accomplished the day's tasks, then left the *bottega* for the Palazzo Medici.

Several months earlier, on one of the rare occasions that Leonardo now saw Ser Piero, his father had told him that the master of the Medici stables was a man from Vinci. Since Ser Piero had once done the man's family a great favor, he was sure the man would not mind if Leonardo spent time at the stables, sketching the Medici's magnificent herd. In fact, the man, whose name was Giorgione, was more than happy to repay Ser Piero's kindnesses.

When Leonardo arrived at the stables, he found Giorgione sitting on a pile of hay in front of one of the stable stalls, stroking the back of a tiny kitten.

"What do you have there, Giorgione?" Leonardo asked as he joined Giorgione on the hay.

"This is my little Gina," Giorgione replied. "Her mother was stepped on by one of the stallions this morning, so I am now her mother."

Leonardo reached out and cupped Gina under her chin. Gina purred softly and then licked one of Leonardo's fingers with her tiny pink tongue.

"She likes you, too, Leonardo," Giorgione

said. He handed Leonardo the kitten and stood up. "You be her mother while I tend to the horses."

Within minutes, Leonardo had forgotten why he had come to the stables. From his knapsack he took out an ink pen and some paper. He placed Gina, who was now sleeping, on the soft hay beside him and started to sketch her. Soon, Leonardo had a very detailed sketch of the tiny animal, curled almost into a ball, her head resting on her left paw, her tail almost touching her nose.

Leonardo eased himself off the straw so he could look at Gina from another angle, and began sketching her from that side. Gina seemed to be dreaming, Leonardo thought, because, from time to time, she would change positions—almost as if she were modeling for Leonardo. It wasn't long until Leonardo had filled several pages of his sketchbook with drawings of the kitten.

Just as Leonardo started to sit back down on the straw and put Gina back in his arms, he noticed a larger cat near another pile of hay a few feet away. She was crouched on all four legs, looking straight at Leonardo as if she were about to spring.

"Are you jealous?" Leonardo asked softly. "Do you want me to draw your picture too?"

The cat continued to stare at Leonardo.

"Well?" Leonardo said.

All of a sudden, the cat stood up and angled her head in profile.

"That's better," Leonardo said.

He turned the page of his notebook and started sketching the new cat. In Leonardo's eyes, this cat really did look like one of its ancestors, so Leonardo let his pen run away with him, and soon the sketch turned into a furious lion. He was pleased with what had just happened.

"Now, then, let's see what you look like when you're angry," Leonardo said to the cat.

With his pen, Leonardo sketched the cat with her back humped and her hair standing on end.

"You are a very good model," Leonardo said. "I see all kinds of things when I look at you."

Leonardo had just finished a third sketch of the cat, this one of her washing herself, when she was scared away by Giogione returning with one of the stallions that Lorenzo de' Medici had been riding that morning.

Leonardo stood up. "What a beautiful animal," he said. "I want to draw him."

Gina meowed, and Leonardo picked her up.

"She was a good girl, so I drew some pictures of her," Leonardo said, showing his notebook to Giorgione. "We had a visitor, too, and I was able to get a few drawings of her."

Giorgione took the notebook from Leonardo and looked at the sketches. "They are so real, I think I will be scratched if I'm not careful," he said.

Leonardo laughed. He handed Gina to Giorgione. "If I don't make some sketches of the horses, then the other apprentices at the *bottega* will be disappointed because it's horses they want to know how to draw, not cats."

For several minutes, Leonardo sketched the stallion from as many angles as he could.

"What a magnificent creature," Leonardo said. "One of these days, Giorgione, I think I shall use these sketches for an equestrian statue."

"And when I see it, Leonardo, I shall remember the day it started as a scratch of your ink pen on paper," Giorgione said.

When Leonardo returned to the *bottega* late that afternoon, Guiliamo and Cicanchi were just coming out the front door.

"What's going on?" Leonardo asked. "Why are you two in such a hurry?"

"We're having a party tonight, Leonardo," Guiliamo said. "We're off to get the wine and the sausages and the bread."

"Do you want to come with us?" Cicanchi asked.

Leonardo grinned. He had something else

in mind. "No, I think I'll stay here and invent some riddles and funny stories," he said.

"Oh, that will be wonderful," Guiliamo shouted over his shoulder. "You do that better than anyone else."

Leonardo went inside the *bottega* and headed up to his room. He couldn't think of a better way to end the day than with a party surrounded by good friends and good food.

There were times when Leonardo wondered why he often felt unhappy when he should have felt happy and felt happy when he should have felt unhappy. He didn't understand how his moods could change so abruptly during the course of a few hours. He only hoped that he could enjoy the entire party that night and that midway through he wouldn't suddenly want to be alone.

Leonardo was glad that Pandolfo wasn't in the room now. He didn't want any distractions. He lay down on his bed and stared up at the ceiling. As always, he saw the cracks as roads, leading to other places. In his mind, he traveled them, meeting people and absorbing everything he could. Often he met people who shared their stories and riddles. When he finally returned to Florence, to the *bottega,* to the room he shared with Pandolfo, he always felt refreshed—like a totally new person.

Domenico came to the door of the room and said, "Well, you're finally awake, friend. Why don't you come on downstairs? People are asking for you."

"In a minute," Leonardo said. He yawned. "In a minute."

After Domenico left, Leonardo sat up and rubbed his eyes. He didn't remember falling asleep. He had been talking to . . . suddenly, he jumped up. He had to act before he forgot what the man had told him.

On one of the roads, during his dreams, Leonardo had met a man who had simply called himself "the prankster."

"Oh, I think you and I could be great friends," Leonardo had told him. "I love playing tricks on people at parties, and I should be very happy if you would share some of your pranks with me."

The prankster had gladly obliged him.

"Leonardo! Leonardo!" several people shouted when Leonardo appeared at the bottom of the steps. "Come join us!"

"Shortly," Leonardo said.

Leonardo went into a room at the back of the *bottega* where Verrocchio kept a lot of supplies. He put the things he needed under his cloak and rejoined the party.

Within minutes, Leonardo awed the crowd by making multicolored flames jump from a cup of boiling oil when he poured red wine into it.

After that, he broke a stick balanced on two glasses without cracking the glasses.

When everyone cried for more tricks, Leonardo said, "Oh, no! Now, I want to sing!"

After everyone had quieted down, Leonardo, accompanying himself on the *lira da braccio*, a viol that he had taught himself to play, sang a song another apprentice had written especially for him.

At midnight, Leonardo went up to his room, then returned and said, "Now I want to show you what the well-dressed apprentice in Florence should be wearing."

For the next hour, Leonardo donned several caps and turbans of bright colors, shirts adorned with lace and embroidery, and close-fitting doublets and hose.

"Bravo!" the apprentices shouted.

Bartolomeo sniffed the air. "And what, pray tell, does the well-dressed apprentice in Florence put on to make himself smell so good?"

Leonardo smiled. "He first takes some fresh rose water and moistens his hands with it," he said. "Then he rubs some lavender flowers between his palms." Leonardo sniffed his hands. "It is very agreeable," he added. Leonardo's face suddenly took on a serious look. "He who wishes to see how the soul inhabits the body should look to see how that body uses its daily surroundings," he said. "If the dwelling is dirty and neglected, the soul will be kept by its body in the same condition, dirty and neglected."

"Ah, our friend here has suddenly turned serious on us," Uziello said. "I do believe . . ."

Verrocchio had appeared at the edge of the group. "It is late, and this dwelling, this *bottega*, is somewhat dirty and neglected, too," he said, "so I think it is about time that we end the merriment and clean up the shop so that we can be ready to work in the morning."

As Leonardo helped the rest of the apprentices get the shop ready to open for business in the morning, he couldn't help wonder, as Uziello had pointed out, how he could have swung so suddenly from being so happy to being so serious. He only wished he understood himself better.

CHAPTER NINE

THE TERRIFYING SHIELD

"Leonardo!"

Leonardo heard Verrocchio calling him from downstairs.

"I'll be right there," Leonardo shouted back. He turned to Pandolfo, who was buttoning up his tunic. "What can the artists' guild really do to help us artists?" he asked. "Their members march in religious processions and, once in a while, they take disciplinary action against someone if he tries to substitute cheap Prussian blue for the more expensive ultramarine. It's all rather silly to me."

Pandolfo shrugged. "What would I know, Leonardo?" he said. "You're the one who'll probably be asked to be a member, not I."

"Leonardo!" Verrocchio shouted again.

"Why does he keep yelling at me?" Leonardo muttered. He yawned. "I wish I could lie back down and get some more sleep, but I'd better go see what he wants."

Leonardo left his room and went downstairs. At the bottom step, he stopped. His father was standing in the middle of the *bottega*, talking to Verrocchio.

"Father!" Leonardo shouted. He hurried over and embraced Ser Piero.

"It's good to see you, Son," Ser Piero said.

"I'm sorry it took me so long," Leonardo said. "I was trying to help Pandolfo figure out the answer to an important question."

"Your father has something he wants to discuss with you, Leonardo," Verrocchio said. "I'll leave you two to conduct your business."

Leonardo turned back to this father. *"Business?"* he said.

Ser Piero nodded. "Do you remember Angelo, one of the sharecroppers on the estate in Vinci?" he asked.

Leonardo had to think for a minute, which surprised him, because it never occurred to him that he could ever forget anything or anyone connected with his childhood. Finally, after having dredged his memory, he came up with the image of a young boy who had once given him a small wooden horse that he said his father had carved for him.

"The carver?" Leonardo asked.

"Yes," Ser Piero replied.

"I have a story to tell you," Leonardo said. He related the incident of the wooden horse. "I buried it under a tree across the road from our house, because I was afraid that Uncle Francesco would make me return it, and I didn't want to." Leonardo took a deep breath and let it out. "It was such a beautiful horse. I wonder if it's still under that tree in Vinci." Leonardo looked at his father and saw by the frown on his face that he wasn't there to hear Leonardo reminisce, so he quickly came back to the present and said, "I'm sorry, Father."

Ser Piero cleared his throat. "When I was in Vinci recently, to talk to your uncle Francesco about estate matters, Angelo came to visit me," he said. "He wanted to ask a favor."

"Surely he didn't want you to tell him where I buried the wooden horse?" Leonardo said.

Ser Piero raised an eyebrow and said, "Verrocchio tells me you're quite the jokester, Leonardo. Of course, some levity does have its place, but I need to talk to you seriously about a commission."

Leonardo could feel himself flushing. He was sure he was beginning to look like a fool in his father's eyes, and that pained him. He was so used to joking around with Verrocchio and the rest of the apprentices that he had almost forgotten how to behave like a son to a father. "I'm sorry," he said.

"No matter, Leonardo," Ser Piero said.

Yet Leonardo was sure that it *did* matter. His father was not here to talk to Leonardo about family matters. Although he was related by blood to the man standing before him, his father was here because Leonardo was an artist. "Pray tell me how I can help you with this matter," Leonardo said.

"Angelo had carved a round shield out of the wood from a fig tree," Ser Piero said. "He asked me if I could have a painter in Florence decorate it for him." Ser Piero picked up the wooden shield. It had been lying on a table behind his father, but Leonardo hadn't noticed it. "As you can see, Son, it's a rather crude job, but Angelo promised to pay me in fish and game, so I told him I would look into it. Naturally, I thought of you, not only because of the reputation you have achieved, but"—Ser Piero smiled—"oh, yes, Leonardo, your accomplishments *do* get back to our house, even if you don't appear often to tell us what you're doing." Ser Piero reached out and touched Leonardo's shoulder. "Verrocchio tells me that it is always good to have fresh fish and game in the *bottega* to feed his hungry apprentices."

Leonardo was finding it hard to breathe.

Had his father just told him, in so many words, that he should come by the house in the Via Larga more often? Was he, Leonardo, the one who was guilty of denying his family his presence?

"I know you're busy, Leonardo," Ser Piero said, returning to the commission at hand, "but do you think you can do something with this?"

Leonardo turned the shield over and over in his hands. It was crudely carved and now badly warped, but he could visualize the changes he could make to produce a work of art. "Yes, Father, I can," he said finally. "Antonio will be very happy with his shield, and those of us who live in this *bottega* will eat very well for several days."

Now that the reason Ser Piero had come to the *bottega* had been taken care of, Leonardo wanted to talk to his father about spending more time with the family, but Ser Piero said, "I must go now, Leonardo. There are business matters that I need to take care of before my family and I leave for Rome." He embraced Leonardo and kissed him on both cheeks, but he said nothing about Leonardo's accompanying them to Rome.

Perhaps I misunderstood his intentions after all, Leonardo thought as he watched his father leave the *bottega. Perhaps no one there really considers me part of the family.*

At that moment, the rest of the apprentices came downstairs. They were all laughing and making faces at Bartolomeo, who had a big grin on his face.

This is my family, Leonardo thought. *I always need to remember that.*

Leonardo took the shield to the kiln in the back of the shop to see if he could reshape the shield by heating it.

Over the next few days, with Uziello's help, the wood began to yield to the heat, so that Leonardo, by using wooden mallets, was able to get rid of the warping.

"I like working with wood from fig trees," Uziello told him. "It speaks to me in special ways, telling me exactly how it wants to look when it's finished."

"I've never talked to a fig tree before," Leonardo said. "I hope this particular piece of wood treats me as kindly as you have been treated."

"Now, what do you plan to do?" Uziello asked him.

"Well, after I polish it, I'm going to varnish it," Leonardo replied.

"Ah, and I suppose you're going to use your secret varnish," Uziello said. "When are you going to let the rest of us know what your formula is?"

"I haven't decided," Leonardo said. "I suppose when I see a creation that deserves the varnish, then I'll offer it, but probably not until then."

"Well, I hope that one of us can measure up to Leonardo's famous varnish," Uziello said jokingly.

★ ★ ★ ★

Two days later, Leonardo felt that the shield was ready to be painted, but what he planned to put on it, he still hadn't decided.

"I'm stumped," Leonardo told Pandolfo that night, after they had both gone to bed. "I've never been this confused before."

"Do you think it's because you're doing it for your father?" Pandolfo asked. "From what you've told me, Leonardo, he seems to intimidate you."

For a minute, Leonardo was silent, but then he said, "I think you may be right, Pandolfo, although I don't like to think that anyone can intimidate me."

"You just want his approval, Leonardo," Pandolfo said, "and there's nothing wrong with that."

"I don't want to talk about it anymore," Leonardo said. He turned over to face the wall.

He was still awake, though, when he heard Pandolfo's gentle snores.

* * * *

The next morning, everything had fallen into place.

"Wake up, Pandolfo!" Leonardo said, shaking his friend's shoulder. "I have it!"

Pandolfo opened his eyes. "What are you talking about?" he asked sleepily. "Why don't you leave me be?"

"No, no, I must tell someone my idea right away, and you're the nearest person," Leonardo said. "When I am finished with this shield, a warrior will only have to show it in battle for his enemies to flee from him in terror."

"Okay, okay, that's wonderful," Pandolfo said. But when Pandolfo tried to turn over, to go back to sleep, Leonardo wouldn't let him.

"Today, I'm going out into the countryside and collect as many lizards as I can find," Leonardo continued. "Yes, yes, yes, that's what I'm going to do." Leonardo was now sitting on the side of Pandolfo's bed and bouncing up and down. "I'll also need some crickets and some snakes and some grass-hoppers and some bats!" Leonardo forced Pandolfo to sit up. "Tell me, my friend, are you not already terrified just thinking about what this shield will look like when it's used in battle?"

"Oh, yes, of course, Leonardo," Pandolfo said. "That's exactly what I'm thinking."

"I don't believe you, Pandolfo, but that's all right," Leonardo said, jumping up from the bed and dressing hurriedly, "because I have already decided that that is exactly how I plan to make the shield."

For the next several weeks, Leonardo worked in almost total secrecy. He collected as many strange creatures as he could find and brought them back to the *bottega*, putting them in one of the storage rooms so he could dissect them, remove their skeletons, and then combine their bones to create a spine-chilling monster.

Leonardo had earlier painted craggy rocks on the shield in such a way that when he fastened the monster onto the wood, it looked as though it were emerging angrily from a cleft, its eyes blazing, its nostrils pouring forth smoke, and fire erupting from its mouth.

Finally, Leonardo was ready. He sent a younger apprentice to his father's house with the message that he had finished the shield and that his father should come by the *bottega* to get it. So that his father wouldn't think he was impertinent with such a demand, Leonardo instructed the apprentice to tell him that Leonardo wasn't feeling well enough to leave the *bottega*.

When the apprentice returned, he said, "Your father will be here within the hour."

"That's perfect. Thank you," Leonardo said. "When my father arrives, please show him to this storeroom."

Leonardo propped the shield up on an easel, then he turned off the lights in the room, adjusted the shutters so that a ray of sunlight fell on his creation, and waited.

Ser Piero arrived as promised.

When he opened the door to the storeroom, he gasped.

"Did it scare you, Father?" Leonardo asked from the gloom of the room.

"Yes! I thought I was suddenly being visited by the devil," Ser Piero said.

"Then take the shield to Antonio, Father, because that is exactly what I had hoped to create," Leonardo said. "Something that would terrify the enemy!"

For the next several weeks, Leonardo was happier than he had been in years, because he felt as though he had really pleased his father. He wanted to visit his father, to ask him what Antonio's reaction to the shield had been, but he didn't want to bother him. He knew that, in good time, Ser Piero would again visit the *bottega* and Leonardo would learn the answer then.

One day, as Pandolfo and Leonardo were walking along the Via della Colonna, looking in the windows of the various shops, Leonardo saw on a shelf a shield that looked almost exactly like the one he had made.

"Pandolfo! How could that be?" Leonardo said. He grabbed the sleeve of his friend's cloak. "I have to find out what is going on here."

Inside the shop, Leonardo approached the shelf, lifted the shield, and began examining it. "This is *my* shield, Pandolfo," Leonardo said, barely above a whisper. He was finding it hard to breathe. "How did it get—"

"Careful there, young man," a voice called from the back of the shop. "I paid one hundred ducats for that shield, and it's not for sale. So please put it down."

"It is a beautiful piece of work," Leonardo said, finding it almost impossible to keep the anger out of his voice. "I should like to visit with the artist, to find out exactly how it was made."

"You'll have to talk to the artist's father," the merchant said. "He's the one who sold it to me, because he said he needed the money."

Leonardo gently replaced the shield on the shelf. "I think that man was not telling you the truth, sir," he said to the merchant. "I can't imagine a father who would do that to anyone he really thought of as a son."

CHAPTER TEN
MAESTRO

On the morning of March 12, 1476, Leonardo opened his eyes with a start. Pandolfo was shaking his shoulders violently.

"What's wrong?" Leonardo asked groggily.

"I've just come from downstairs. There are two Officers of the Night talking to Verrocchio," Pandolfo whispered. "Someone has filed a complaint against you."

Leonardo sat up. "Who would do such a thing?" he demanded.

"People do this in secret, Leonardo," Pandolfo said. "No one ever signs his name to the letter."

Leonardo got out of bed and dressed hurriedly. "I've done nothing wrong, Pandolfo," he said. "I need to set this matter straight right away. I can't have my reputation ruined by lies."

"It doesn't matter," Pandolfo reminded him. "If someone accuses you, it has to be investigated."

Leonardo knew that Pandolfo was right about this. All around Florence, there were *buchi della Veritá*—"mouths of truth"—special mailboxes that allowed people to complain about other people anonymously. Everyone knew that these mailboxes made it very easy for people to denounce neighbors they didn't like as thieves or murderers. Once a complaint was made, it had to be investigated by the appropriate authority in the city.

"But why are the Officers of the Night here?" Leonardo asked. "They are only concerned with moral behavior."

Pandolfo shrugged. "Perhaps the husband of one of your female clients thought you were too friendly with his wife," he said.

"I find that insulting," Leonardo said. "I am always very proper with my female clients.

I would never do anything that would offend someone."

"It doesn't have to be the truth, Leonardo. You know that," Pandolfo said. "It's mostly a way for people to get even with other people."

Leonardo had finished dressing. "I can't imagine who I would have angered enough for him to do something like this to me," he said. Leonardo felt the tears welling up in his eyes. "If I only had someone I could . . ." He stopped, unable to continue.

Pandolfo embraced him. "You do have someone, Leonardo," he said. "In fact, you have everyone in the *bottega*. We're all the family you need."

Leonardo swallowed hard and pulled away from Pandolfo's embrace. "I know, and I try always to remember that, Pandolfo, but it's just that . . . I sometimes wish that I had a father and a mother and brothers and sisters who would, at a time like this, embrace me and tell me that everything will be all right." He wiped away the tears and took a deep breath. "But I know this is no time to start feeling sorry for myself."

Leonardo left the room and went downstairs.

The two Officers of the Night were standing at the entrance to the *bottega*, but Verrocchio had already started toward the stairs, when he saw Leonardo.

"I was just coming to get you, Leonardo," Verrocchio said in a normal voice. He had a solemn expression on his face. "There are two gentlemen here who need to talk to you." When he reached Leonardo, he whispered, "Do not admit anything to them until you have had a chance to talk to a notary."

"I have nothing to hide," Leonardo whispered back, "but I shall do as you say."

Together, Leonardo and Verrocchio approached the two stern-looking officers.

I shall survive this, Leonardo told himself. *I shall not allow anyone to ruin my life.*

Along with three other young men, Leonardo was accused of associating with Jacopo Saltarelli, a known street criminal.

"That is a lie!" Leonardo said. "I did not and would not do such a thing!"

"Do you know this Jacopo Saltarelli?" one of the officers asked.

Leonardo blushed. "I know his name, because he is notorious in Florence," he finally replied. "It is not unusual for people to talk about people like that." He looked the two men in the eye. "Have you never talked about the notorious people of Florence? I think you have. I think we all have."

Leonardo could tell that both officers were angered by his challenges, so he decided that he had said enough.

"Be that as it may," one officer said between clinched teeth, "you have been accused of wrongful behavior, and you are hereby commanded to appear before the judge of the Court of Inquiry on April ninth."

With that, the two officers turned and left the *bottega.*

"You must tell me the truth, Leonardo," Verrocchio said. "Did this happen?"

Leonardo looked Verrocchio straight in the eye. "No, it did not," he said.

"I believe you," Verrocchio said. "This morning, I shall talk to several people on your behalf. They will be able to help you."

As Verrocchio started to leave, Leonardo grasped the sleeve of his cloak. "Should I tell my father about this?" he asked.

Without hesitating, Verrocchio said, "At this time, Leonardo, I think not." He gently put his hand on Leonardo's shoulder. "Later, perhaps, but this is not something that I think your father would want to worry about now."

The first hearing produced no results. The law required that there be firm evidence and signed statements from witnesses for the complaint. None were forthcoming, so Leonardo and the three other young men were discharged and told that they had to return for another hearing on June 7. Once again, no evidence against Leonardo and the other young men was produced, so the judge dismissed the case.

That night, at the *bottega*, when everyone was celebrating the end of Leonardo's troubles, Verrocchio stood up and said, "This should be a lesson, though, to all of you. There are people outside this happy little family who think nothing about destroying a person's reputation. When you are dealing with people you do not know very well, you should always remember that."

It was a lesson that Leonardo would remember the rest of his life.

Later that night, after everyone had already gone to bed, Leonardo told a sleepy Pandolfo, "I suppose this is easy to say now, my friend, but this affair has stirred something in me that makes me want to create a masterpiece."

Pandolfo yawned. "How could such an awful experience do that?" he asked.

"The charges weren't true, Pandolfo, but if something *had* happened and some witnesses had appeared and made everyone believe them, then I could have been sent to prison," Leonardo said. "It made me think about what

I would not have been able to accomplish with the rest of my life. I realized what a waste that would be of the things I know I can do but which I've put off just because I thought I had plenty of time to do them."

This time, only Pandolfo's snoring answered him, so Leonardo turned over on his side and tried to go to sleep himself. But he couldn't relax, so he got out of bed, left the room, and walked to the end of the darkened hallway, where a narrow window looked out onto the street below. The moon was full, and Leonardo stood and watched the sleeping city, wondering about the lives of the people within the other buildings and how they were all connected to one another in some way. In his mind, he wove these relationships into an intricate pattern, which proved his theory that everything in the world was somehow connected to everything else.

Finally, near dawn, Leonardo crawled back into his bed. When Pandolfo's stirring awakened him, Leonardo knew that he had only been asleep for a few minutes, but he couldn't remember ever having felt so rested.

Leonardo went downstairs at the same time as several of the other apprentices, thinking that he would be working with them on a float for an upcoming parade. But Verrocchio pulled him aside and said, "Stand with me. I want to make an announcement."

Verrocchio clapped his hands and called the rest of the apprentices before him.

"Leonardo has now been with me for over ten years, as you know, and in that time he has accomplished more than I could ever have imagined," Verrocchio said. "In that time, though, Leonardo is not the only one who has prospered. I, Andrea del Verrocchio, and all of you are better artists because of the young man standing beside me." Verrocchio looked at Leonardo. "You are now a *maestro* in your own right. I have tendered your application for membership to the artists' guild, and it has been accepted."

The apprentices broke into applause. Several shouted, *"Bravo! Bravo!"*

Leonardo smiled. "Thank you," he said. "Thank you very, very much."

"Now, it's back to work for all of us," Verrocchio said unceremoniously.

Just as Leonardo started to rejoin the rest of the apprentices, Verrocchio pulled him back once again and said, "No, no, I have another job for you. Amerigo de' Benci just left the shop, Leonardo. He wants a portrait painted of his daughter, Ginevra. I want you to do it."

"Ah, yes, I know the family. Amerigo is a very wealthy banker," Leonardo said. "I am friends with Ginevra's cousin Tommaso and her brother Giovanni. I have on occasion lent them some of my books."

Verrocchio nodded. "This will be a very good commission for you, Leonardo, and perhaps the start of your becoming a wealthy artist instead of just a poor apprentice."

All of a sudden, it occurred to Leonardo that as a *maestro* he might be expected to move to his own *bottega* and take on his own apprentices, something he didn't want to do. He wanted to stay where he was.

Almost as if he had read Leonardo's mind, Verrocchio said, "I count on you for many, many things, Leonardo, and I would be very pleased if you would consider remaining here for a while—in fact, for as long as you want." Verrocchio paused. "Of course, if you would prefer—"

"This is my home, Verrocchio," Leonardo said, interrupting him. "I'm not ready to leave yet."

"Good! That's settled," Verrocchio said. "We'll discuss it no more until you bring up the matter yourself."

"Agreed," Leonardo said.

Over the next several months, Leonardo was at the Benci estate almost daily. He couldn't remember ever having enjoyed himself so much. Ginevra was not only a beautiful woman but was also a writer of poetry, and often during her sittings she would recite her latest poem for Leonardo and ask him what he thought about it.

When the portrait was finally finished, Verrocchio said, "It is not a portrait, Leonardo, it is Ginevra in person."

The rest of Florence agreed. The entire landscape, which surrounded Ginevra de' Benci, seemed to develop from her: the leaves of the juniper, the twilight sky, the flicker of the waters, the distant blue of the sky. They merged with one another.

"What do you call this, Leonardo?" several artists asked him at the unveiling of the portrait.

"It's a *sfumato* effect," Leonardo told them. "I see everything as sort of evaporating into smoke."

"Interesting, interesting," the artists said as they crowded in to get a closer look.

"I've been experimenting with the discontinuity of matter," Leonardo explained. "I wanted to break up the shapes. I wanted the contours to disappear. I wanted the landscape and the figure to merge."

"Amazing, simply amazing," everyone said.

Inwardly, Leonardo smiled. All of a sudden, he remembered that this was exactly what had been said to him many years ago by his grandfather, Father Enzo, and Verrocchio: *Amazing, simply amazing.*

I do feel like a maestro *now,* he thought. *I really do.*

CHAPTER ELEVEN

SAVING LORENZO DE' MEDICI

Occasionally, at a time when he thought Ser Piero would be leaving, Leonardo would intentionally walk past the government building where his father worked. Leonardo, always making sure he was in the company of a friend, would act as if the whole thing had been a chance encounter.

Even after several of these "chance" encounters within just a short period of time, it never occurred to Ser Piero that his son was doing this on purpose.

Leonardo, himself, wasn't even sure why he was doing it. After the discovery that his father had lied to him about the shield, he had never quite felt the same about him. Still, deep down, there was a familial pull that Leonardo couldn't ignore.

On this day, Leonardo had just bought Giuliamo some ice cream, when he heard his father say, "Leonardo! We see each other again."

Leonardo looked up, feigning surprise, and said, "Oh, how are you, Father?"

"Well," Ser Piero said.

Leonardo knew about his father's new wife and another son, who had been named Antonio, after Leonardo's grandfather, but he decided not to inquire about them. Instead, he asked, "How are things at the Palazzo Medici?"

His father's face darkened. "There are intrigues everywhere, as always, Leonardo, and sometimes I think that I should take my family back to Vinci. But I have put my faith in Lorenzo, and I do believe that he is more than capable of keeping Florence as a great power." Ser Piero suddenly looked around, as if he had just realized that someone else might be listening to him. "Of course, I am telling you all of this in the strictest of confidences, Leonardo, and I warn you and your friend here not to repeat what you just heard."

"Of course not, Father," Leonardo said. "You have my word that politics simply doesn't interest me."

Leonardo was telling his father the truth. He had heard things, of course, because some of the other artists talked a lot about the political situation in Italy, which was like a miniature continent in itself. There were five great powers—Venice, Milan, Rome, Naples, and, of course, Florence—all ruled by powerful families that were constantly trying to figure out ways to expand their territories at the expense of one another. Added to this were the smaller, less powerful, cities of Ferrara, Urbino, Genoa, Siena, and Mantua, which were capable of making trouble for the larger cities.

There were some people in Florence who complained about the Medicis, especially the

Pazzi family, who were second in power only to the Medicis. They hated Lorenzo and wanted to see the entire family swept out to the sea. But for most of the people in Florence, Lorenzo was a wonderful ruler.

Of course, a lot of the support for the Medicis came from Lorenzo's having decreed that almost every month Florence would have carnivals or parades or tournaments of some kind. When one event was finished, the people of Florence immediately began preparing for the next event. Most of the citizens were too occupied with having fun to worry about the political intrigues going on behind the walls of the houses of the ruling men.

As usual, Verrocchio and his apprentices, including Leonardo, created the wonderful backdrops and floats for most of these events.

"I have some wonderful ideas for masks, Leonardo," Uziello said one evening. "Would you like to work with me?"

"How can Leonardo work with you, Uziello?" Domenico demanded. "He'll be working with me to make the costumes."

Leonardo laughed. "I can work with both of you," he said. "You know how easily I get bored with one project," he added, making fun of himself.

Within a week, the masks and the costumes, along with the floats and the backdrops for the plays, had been completed and were taken to the various locales around central Florence.

The events took place over several days, and Leonardo, when he wasn't participating, enjoyed watching. By late Saturday afternoon, Leonardo was exhausted from all the festivities and went to bed early.

The early morning bells from *Santa Maria del Fiore* awakened him, which Leonardo thought was strange, because he had never noticed them before.

When he first arrived in Florence, Leonardo attended Mass almost as faithfully as he had in Vinci, but gradually, he went less and less. Often, it was because he was busy with things at the *bottega* or spending Sundays in the countryside. It wasn't long, though, before he not only stopped attending Mass completely but also began to despise the antics of the priests.

When asked about this one morning by Pandolfo as his friend headed out the door for Mass, Leonardo said, "A priest produces many words, receives much wealth, and promises paradise, Pandolfo. But I believe what they all really do is trade in tricks and simulated miracles and dupe the foolish multitudes."

"Leonardo, that is heresy!" Pandolfo said.

"Someone has to unmask them, friend," Leonardo replied. "If I don't, then they would impose this tyranny on everyone."

Pandolfo stormed out of the *bottega* and for days afterward would hardly speak to Leonardo. Finally, Pandolfo approached him one evening and asked, "Leonardo, do you believe in God?"

Without hesitation, Leonardo said, "Of course, I believe in God. I have discovered God in the beauty of light, in the movement of the planets, in the intricate arrangement of muscles and nerves inside the body, and in the masterpiece of the human soul." Leonardo gave Pandolfo a puzzled look. "How could you, as an artist, ask such a question of me?"

After that, Pandolfo acted as if nothing had ever happened between them, but he and Leonardo never again talked about religion.

On this morning, though, Leonardo felt himself being pulled to the cathedral, as if in a dream. He got out of bed as quietly as he could, not wanting to be questioned by Pandolfo about where he was going.

When Leonardo was dressed, he crept downstairs and left the *bottega* without being noticed.

As Leonardo approached the cathedral, he saw the most important and most powerful people in Florence going inside for Mass. At the rear of the throng were his father and his new stepmother.

Leonardo hid in a doorway so his parents

wouldn't see him. When only a few stragglers remained, he headed toward the cathedral.

Suddenly, a carriage pulled up in front. Lorenzo de' Medici and his brother Giuliano alighted and hurried up the steps of the main entrance.

Once again, Leonardo held back. For some reason, he suddenly felt unworthy sitting in the midst of the most powerful people in Florence, and that angered him.

I don't feel this way when I'm painting or drawing or making furniture for these people, he told himself. *Why should I feel that way now?*

Leonardo wanted to turn around and run back to the *bottega*, to the security of his small room, jump into bed, and cover up his head with his covers. But the pull he had felt that morning when the morning bells had awakened him was still there, and he felt himself being drawn unwillingly toward the cathedral.

When Leonardo reached the front door, though, he stopped and decided that the only way he could get through the service would be to watch it unobserved.

He found a door with steps leading up to a small window where he knew he could look out onto the congregation.

The priest's incantations and the music made his heart sing, and for the duration of the Mass, Leonardo was transported back to his childhood in Vinci.

When the bell sounded at the end of the service, Leonardo started to turn, but he suddenly noticed light flashing off the blade of a drawn sword. He instinctively knew that something awful was about to happen to the Medici brothers and that he had to do something about it.

As Leonardo fled down the steps, he heard shouts and screams coming from the people as they tried to escape the cathedral.

When Leonardo reached the bottom step, he turned to his right, a direction he knew would take him along the sides of the sanctuary but which would also keep him in darkness, as he made his way toward where the battle was being fought.

When Leonardo reached the front of the sanctuary he saw that Lorenzo and Giuliano were fighting for their lives against several members of the Pazzi family.

Suddenly, one of the Pazzis hurled himself on Giuliano and started stabbing him with his sword. Lorenzo, his throat bleeding from a wound, was doing his best to defend himself. When Lorenzo managed to knock the sword out of the hands of one of his attackers, it gave him a chance to escape. Leonardo saw him look painfully at what was happening to Giuliano, but realizing there was no way he could help his brother, Lorenzo raced for the sacristy and managed to shut and lock the double bronze doors.

Leonardo knew he had to act right away. Sooner or later, the Pazzis and their allies would find some way to break into the sacristy. Still in the shadows, staying as close to the sides of the wall as he could, Leonardo raced back toward the steps he had just come down. Over the years he had been in Florence, if there was one building he knew every inch of, it was *Santa Maria del Fiore.* Leonardo had studied its architecture, its frescoes, its paintings—everything—so he knew how to get into the sacristy from another part of the cathedral.

When he reached the top of the steps, he turned to his right. He quickly wove his way through dark passageways, musty rooms, and down a narrow staircase until he reached a small wooden door. He opened it quietly. Below him, he saw Lorenzo, one hand pressed against the bronze doors, the other hand pressed against the bleeding wound on his neck.

"Signore!" Leonardo called.

Lorenzo looked up, startled.

"I am your friend," Leonardo said. "Let me help you escape."

Lorenzo hesitated, then he took his hand from the door, but he kept his other hand on his neck wound and stayed where he was.

"I am not one of them," Leonardo said. "If you stack up those boxes in the corner, I think I can reach your hand and pull you up."

As the pounding on the doors got louder, Lorenzo took a deep breath and said, "I have no other choice. I have to trust you."

When Lorenzo took his hand away from his neck wound, blood started streaming down onto his shirt, but he began stacking the boxes to make stair steps so he could climb to the top of them.

Leonardo leaned down from the small opening as far as he could and was finally able to grasp Lorenzo's fingertips. Slowly, he began pulling the powerful leader of Florence to safety.

Suddenly, from behind him, Leonardo heard the voices of several men. He knew if they belonged to the Pazzis, both he and Lorenzo would be killed.

"Lorenzo!" a voice called. "It's Enrico!"

"That's my cousin," Lorenzo managed to gasp. "You must get him to help us."

"Enrico!" Leonardo called. "In here."

As three men came down the small passageway, the one in front said, "Who are you? Where is Lorenzo de' Medici?"

"In the sacristy," Leonardo told them. "I'm trying to pull him up, but I need your help."

Two of the men were able to crowd in on both sides of Leonardo and grasp Lorenzo's arms. In minutes, he had been pulled into the small room and a bandage had been made, from the sleeve of one of the men's shirts, and was wound around his neck to stop the bleeding.

Lorenzo embraced Leonardo. "I shall never forget this," he said.

"Come, Lorenzo, we mustn't tarry," Enrico said. "The wound needs to be dressed, and you need to get back to the palace for your safety."

"What about the people?" Lorenzo asked. "I heard the bells. Are they heeding the Pazzis' cry for liberation?"

"No, not at all," one of the other men said. "They have taken your side unanimously, and

they are at this very moment pursuing the conspirators."

Without another word, Lorenzo left with
the three men and Leonardo was all alone in
the small room above the sacristy. He leaned
against the wall, wondering if God had called
him that morning to help save Lorenzo de'
Medici's life. He didn't know what the answer
was. Finally, exhausted, both physically and
emotionally, Leonardo returned to the *bottega*
and, careful not to wake the still sleeping
Pandolfo, crawled into bed and went back to
sleep.

The conspirators—including some priests—
were hunted down and before long their corpses
were hanging from poles all around Florence.
By decree, the Pazzi name was banned from the
city and the family's coat of arms was removed
from every building where it had been.

As was usual in such cases of high treason
against the state, a painter was commissioned
to depict the hanging of the guilty men on the

facade of the Bargello prison—which happened to be just around the corner from Ser Piero's house—to frighten any remaining Pazzi supporters into submission.

Verrecchio approached Leonardo about the work, saying that it was his if he wanted it. But it reminded Leonardo of just how terribly cruel human beings could be to one another, and he turned Verrocchio down.

"I am not interested," Leonardo told him. "I do not want to think about such an awful thing."

CHAPTER TWELVE

GOOD-BYE TO FLORENCE

"I handle the legal affairs for the friars of Abbey San Donato at Scopeto, Leonardo," Ser Piero said, "and I have been able to obtain a commission for you for an altarpiece that is to represent the adoration of the Magi."

Leonardo knew that Scopeta was a small town just outside Florence. "Thank you, Father. I shall do my best," he said stiffly. "What amount of money will I receive from the good monks for doing this work?"

Ser Piero shifted from one foot to the other. "It is an unusual contract, Leonardo, but in the end, you will benefit greatly from it."

"What do you mean, *unusual*?" Leonardo asked.

Ser Piero cleared his throat. "The monks

have no money, but a wealthy merchant in the area, Paolo Voghiera, left them his estate on the condition that they provide a dowry for his daughter, Lisabetta. As payment for your work, you will receive one third of the estate. But you may do nothing with the land for three years, and the abbey can buy the land back from you at any time for three hundred florins."

"That is a very large amount," Leonardo agreed.

Ser Piero cleared his throat once again. "There is a final stipulation, though," he said. "You are to provide one hundred fifty florins for this girl's dowry, and you will also pay for your own paints and gold leaf."

"I see what you mean by *unusual*, Father," Leonardo said.

Now Ser Piero looked Leonardo directly in the eye. "You must not disappoint me, Son," he said. "You have only thirty months to finish the altarpiece, and if you do not do that in the allotted time, you will forfeit the work done up to that point."

"I shall try not to disappoint you," Leonardo said.

After Leonardo had signed the contract, Ser Piero left the *bottega*, saying that he would let the friars at San Donato know that his famous son had agreed to their terms.

Verrocchio walked up behind him. "I was listening, Leonardo. You are crazy to sign such an agreement," he said. "Why did you do it?"

"It offers me the chance to create a masterpiece, Verrocchio," Leonardo said. "If I finish it, I shall have praise heaped upon me not only by the people of Florence but by everyone in Italy."

"And if you don't finish it?" Verrocchio asked.

Leonardo shrugged. "I don't want to think about that now," he said. He smiled at Verrocchio. "Have you forgotten what today is?" he asked.

Verrocchio clasped his hands together. "Your birthday!" he said. "Of course!"

"Yes, Verrocchio, it's my birthday," Leonardo

said. "The fifteenth of April, 1480. I am twenty-eight years old, and . . ." Leonardo stopped. He suddenly felt a darkness descending heavily upon him. "And I still have to depend on my father to get me commissions that I can't possibly . . ." Leonardo stopped. "I shall do my best, Verrocchio. I shall do my best."

"That's all any of us can do, Leonardo," Verrocchio said.

Before Leonardo began his work on the altarpiece, he looked at some of the studies he had done in 1478 for the *Adoration of the Shepherds* in the San Bernardo chapel in the Signoria, the building that housed the offices of Florence's city-state government, a commission he never completed. But he decided that he had grown since then and that these figures, arranged in a square around the Virgin Mary, wouldn't work for what he now had in mind.

After thinking about the altarpiece for several weeks, day and night, Leonardo told

Verrocchio, "I think I know now what I want to do."

"Tell me, so I can learn from you, Leonardo," Verrocchio said.

"I want to take a familiar scene, the three Wise Men's adoration of Christ, and I want to give it a fresh and lively sprit, even if I have to rewrite the Gospels."

Verrocchio raised an eyebrow, but he didn't say anything.

"I am going to move the manger to the side, which will allow for a crowd of people to surround Mary holding the Christ Child."

"I suppose you have a reason for making this change," Verrocchio said.

"Yes, of course. A good painter has two subjects of primary importance: Man, and the state of Man's mind," Leonardo said. "The first is easy, but the second one is very difficult, because it must be conveyed by gestures and by the movements of the various parts of the body."

"What will I do when you're gone from

here, Leonardo? Who will be around to show us how to recognize what is right in front of our eyes?" Verrocchio asked. "What you say is something that makes sense, yet it is something that no one has ever thought of doing before."

"In religious paintings, the people stand by placidly, Verrocchio, separated from the event taking place," Leonardo continued. "I want the people in my painting to look real, and they will look real only if they are reacting, as real people do, to the magnificent event they are witnessing."

"I have never been more excited about one of your commissions than I am about this one, Leonardo," Verrocchio said. "I honestly think you have reached the point you have been aspiring for."

From time to time, over the next few months, monks from San Donato would visit the *bottega* to check on the progress of the altarpice. They could easily see that Leonardo was creating an exceptional work of art, but they were all concerned that he wasn't working more quickly on it.

In September 1482, the monks sent Leonardo a bushel of wheat and a cask of red wine.

"I think it's a bribe," Leonardo said. "I think they are telling me that, although my thirty months are almost up, I am still in their good graces."

For the next year, Leonardo worked on the altarpiece in between other commissions, but finally in January 1484, after the monks of San Donato started pressuring him to complete the work, he decided that he had had enough of them and of the altarpiece, which he called the *Adoration of the Magi*. He delivered the unfinished painting to the abbey and left it without any explanation as to why he had stopped.

When Leonardo returned to the *bottega*, he went straight to Verrocchio. "I am suffocating in Florence, and I can no longer work in this city," he said. "I will pack my meager belongings tonight and, early in the morning, I shall leave for Milan. There, I hope I shall find my salvation."

Leonardo da Vinci was thirty-one years old.

CHAPTER THIRTEEN

THE LAST SUPPER

In 1484, Leonardo moved to Milan because it was a more diverse city than Florence. He thought it would afford him the opportunity not only to continue his art but to work on scientific and engineering projects as well.

Milan's ruler was Ludovico Sforza. Because of its location, Milan was often a point of military contention among the powerful states of the region, so Leonardo wrote Sforza a letter offering his service as a military engineer. During his years in Milan, Leonardo designed a military tank and a chariot with scythes attached to its wheels.

Leonardo's first major painting in Milan was *Virgin of the Rocks*. Art historians consider it to be a very complex painting. *Portrait of a*

Musician and *Lady with an Ermine* were two other important paintings Leonardo did in the first years after he arrived in Milan.

Leonardo also continued his research into anatomy. His drawings show the structure and the functions of the human body. His discoveries were revolutionary because they contradicted the medical beliefs of the time.

In 1496, Leonardo began work on a large wall painting for Sforza, which he called *The Last Supper.* The painting shows Jesus at his last meal with the disciples before he was arrested and crucified. It is considered one of Leonardo's most famous paintings. While he was working on the wall painting, the famous mathematician Fra Luca Pacioli came to live in Milan. He was in awe of the many designs and discoveries attributed to Leonardo. When Leonardo asked Pacioli to tutor him further in mathematics, Pacioli agreed.

Because some people did not consider Sforza to be the legitimate ruler of Milan, he was eager to erect monuments and statues around the city to remind people of his heritage and authority. He commissioned Leonardo to make a bronze equestrian statue to honor his father. It would stand twenty feet tall and weigh 200,000 pounds. The project took up a great deal of Leonardo's time. He worked on different designs and models for it for almost twenty years.

In 1499, the French invaded Lombardy, the province of which Milan was the capital, and the political situation in the city changed drastically. Sforza fled to Germany. When French soldiers began using Leonardo's equestrian models for crossbow practice, he and Pacioli decided to leave for Mantua. There, Leonardo worked briefly on a portrait of Isabelle d'Este, a patron of the arts, but he never finished the painting.

In early 1500, Leonardo and Pacioli left Mantua for Venice. At the time, Venice was at war with the Ottoman Empire and Leonardo offered his services as an engineer. He told the Senate of Venice that he would be able to construct a mobile dam on the Isonzo River. If the Venetian forces could draw the Turkish army into the river valley, he explained, then the water could be released, wiping out the enemy. In addition, Leonardo designed a diving apparatus, similar to modern scuba gear, that would allow divers to stay under water long enough to drill holes in the Turkish ships. Unfortunately, the Venetians never used any of Leonardo's plans, but Leonardo was careful to keep the designs secret so they wouldn't fall into the wrong hands.

By the end of April 1500, Leonardo had decided to return to Florence.

CHAPTER FOURTEEN

MONA LISA

When Leonardo arrived back in Florence, he went first to his father's house, hoping that Ser Piero, now a very wealthy man of seventy-four years, would be more welcoming, but it wasn't to be. Ser Piero had married his fourth wife, and they didn't seem interested in having Leonardo stay with them.

Leonardo was able to live with the Servite friars on the promise that he would paint an altarpiece of the Virgin Mary and her mother, Saint Anne. Although Leonardo worked on the altarpiece over the years he was back in Florence, he never completed it.

In 1502, Cesare Borgia, who was commander of Pope Alexander VI's army and whom Leonardo had met in Milan, gave

Leonardo another chance to be a military engineer. Borgia had conquered most of central Italy, called the Romagna, and it was Leonardo's job to travel the coast to inspect the fortifications and to drain the marshes. He ended up in Imola, where Borgia had set up his winter quarters. It was while he was in Imola that Leonardo drew what is considered the first overhead map of a city.

Sensing that Cesar Borgia's power would soon come to an end, Leonardo left his post in 1503 and returned to Florence.

In just a couple of years the entire atmosphere of the city had changed. The new republican government wanted to take advantage of Florence's famous son. They commissioned Leonardo to paint the *Battle of Anghiari* on a side wall of the new council hall at the Palazzo della Signoria. This, too, was never completed.

Around 1505, Leonardo started what is perhaps his most famous painting, the *Mona Lisa*—also known as *La Gioconda*. Some art critics believe that it is a female version of

Leonardo, while others think it's the wife of Francesco del Gioconda. The Gioconda family never owned the painting, though. When Leonardo eventually went to France, toward the end of his life, he took the painting with him. Many years later, the French royal family kept the painting. When their palace, the Louvre, was opened up to the public after the French Revolution, the painting became the property of the French people and was available for everyone to see.

In 1506, Charles d'Amboise, the French governor of Lombardy, summoned Leonardo back to Milan. Leonardo was now an international celebrity, and powerful people wanted him to be a part of their circle of friends. The government in Florence was angry, though, and wanted Leonardo to return because he hadn't finished painting the *Battle of Anghiari*. Leonardo ignored their wishes and stayed in Milan because he said he felt more comfortable there.

Leonardo's fortunes began to rise. It wasn't

long before he became court painter and engineer to Louis XII, king of France.

Leonardo's father had died in 1504, and his legitimate sons claimed all of Ser Piero's inheritance. Leonardo couldn't do anything about it. But in 1507, Leonardo had to return to Florence because his uncle Francesco had died and left him a large amount of money. Once again, Leonardo's brothers tried to deprive him of his inheritance, but this time, Leonardo took them to court. The proceedings lasted nearly six months, but Leonardo received his inheritance and went back to Milan.

Over the next several years, Leonardo increased his work in anatomical studies. He sketched every organ in the human body, from many different angles. For the sixteenth century, this was considered a very modern technique. Leonardo also began a serious study of hydraulics.

By 1511, at the age of fifty-nine, Leonardo thought of himself as an old man. He had begun to have jealous rages against some of the young men who studied under him. He found it more and more difficult to produce as much work as he once had. He also felt that he was no longer appreciated, and this often sent him into a deep depression. He knew he needed to make a change in his life, but he was at a loss as to what it should be.

CHAPTER FIFTEEN
DEATH IN FRANCE

In 1512, the political climate in Milan changed, so Leonardo and his pupils decided to go to Rome, where Leo X, the brother of Lorenzo and Giovanni de' Medici, was now pope. They lived in apartments in the Belvedere, a villa inside the walls of the Vatican.

During the three years he was in Rome, Leonardo pursued architecture, hydraulics, and the dynamics of mirrors. His self-portrait, which shows an old man with a long beard and a haggard look, was done through a complex arrangement of mirrors so that Leonardo could see himself at every angle.

While he was in Rome, Leonardo finished his last major painting, *St. John the Baptist.*

In 1515, Leonardo went to Bologna to attend the peace talks between the pope and Francis I, the new king of France. As a peace offering to the king from the Medici family, Leonardo built a mechanical lion that was able to walk a few paces. When the lion stopped, a trapdoor opened in the lion's chest, revealing a fleur-de-lis, the symbol of France. The king was very impressed with what Leonardo had done.

By 1516, Michelangelo, Raphael, and Titian had become the leading artists in Italy, and Leonardo began to believe that he was no longer important in the art world. He decided to accept Francis I's invitation to move to France.

The journey to the Loire Valley took almost three months. Leonardo, with his pupils, loaded several pack animals with chests containing all of Leonardo's belongings—including the *Mona Lisa*. When the group entered France, Leonardo looked back once and said good-bye to his native Italy. He knew he would never return.

When Leonardo and his pupils arrived at Amboise, they took up residence in a magnificent manor at Cloux. It was connected by a short underground tunnel to the king's château. Francis I treated his new guests royally. Although one of Leonardo's arms was now paralyzed, leaving him unable to paint, the king thought having him as part of the French court was worth the expense. Leonardo was regarded as one of the most civilized men in Europe, and Francis I enjoyed his conversation.

In April 1519, Leonardo sensed his death was near, so he drew up his will. He divided a vineyard he owned in Italy among his servants and his pupils. He also gave each of his half brothers some money and the property his uncle Francesco had willed him.

Leonardo da Vinci died on May 2, 1519, at the age of sixty-seven. He had been a painter, a sculptor, and an architect. He had also been a scientist and an inventor who was hundreds of years ahead of his time. In fact, people today still get inspiration from his drawings and his ideas.

Leonardo da Vinci was indeed one of the most amazing people who ever lived.

FOR MORE INFORMATION

BOOKS

Bramly, Serge. *Leonardo: The Artist and the Man.* New York: Penguin Books, 1994.

Byrd, Robert. *Leonardo, Beautiful Dreamer.* New York: Dutton Children's Books, 2003.

Hart, Tony. *Famous Children: Leonardo da Vinci.* Hauppauge, New York: Barron's, 1994.

Herbert, Janis. *Leonardo da Vinci for Kids: His Life and Ideas.* Chicago: Chicago Review Press, 1998.

Stanley, Diane. *Leonardo da Vinci.* New York: William Morrow and Company, Inc., 1996.

Wild, Fiona, Project Editor. *Italy—DK Eyewitness Travel Guides*. New York: DK Publishing, Inc., 2004.

WEB SITES

http://www.mos.org/leonardo/
http://www.leonardo.net/main.html
http://www.leonet.it/comuni/vinci

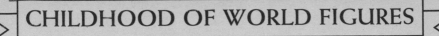

CHILDHOOD OF WORLD FIGURES

CHRISTOPHER COLUMBUS

ANNE FRANK

DIANA, PRINCESS OF WALES

POPE JOHN PAUL II

LEONARDO DA VINCI

COMING SOON:

MOTHER TERESA

★ ★ COLLECT THEM ALL! ★ ★

ALADDIN CLASSICS

ALL THE BEST BOOKS FOR CHILDREN AND THEIR FAMILIES TO READ!

THE SECRET GARDEN
by Frances Hodgson Burnett
Foreword by E. L. Konigsburg
0-689-83141-2

TREASURE ISLAND
by Robert Louis Stevenson
Foreword by Avi
0-689-83212-5

ALICE'S ADVENTURES IN WONDERLAND
by Lewis Carroll
Foreword by Nancy Willard
0-689-83375-X

LITTLE WOMEN
by Louisa May Alcott
Foreword by Joan W. Blos
0-689-83531-0

THE HOUND OF THE BASKERVILLES
by Sir Arthur Conan Doyle
Foreword by Bruce Brooks
0-689-83571-X

THE WIND IN THE WILLOWS
by Kenneth Grahame
Foreword by Susan Cooper
0-689-83140-4

THE WIZARD OF OZ
by L. Frank Baum
Foreword by Eloise McGraw
0-689-83142-0

THE ADVENTURES OF HUCKLEBERRY FINN
by Mark Twain
Foreword by Gary Paulsen
0-689-83139-0

ALADDIN CLASSICS

THE CALL OF THE WILD
by Jack London
Foreword by Gary Paulsen
0-689-85674-1

HEIDI
by Johanna Spyri
Foreword by Eloise McGraw
0-689-83962-6

*THE RAVEN AND OTHER
WRITINGS*
by Edgar Allan Poe
Foreword by Avi
0-689-86352-7

A CHRISTMAS CAROL
by Charles Dickens
Foreword by Nancy Farmer
0-689-87180-5

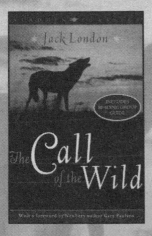

PETER PAN
by J.M. Barrie
Foreword by Susan Cooper
0-689-86691-7

ANNE OF GREEN GABLES
by L. M. Montgomery
Foreword by Katherine Paterson
0-689-84622-3

A LITTLE PRINCESS
by Frances Hodgson Burnett
Foreword by Nancy Bond
0-689-84407-7

UNCLE TOM'S CABIN
by Harriet Beecher Stowe
Foreword by
Christopher Paul Curtis
0-689-85126-X

★ ★ ★ Childhood of Famous Americans ★ ★ ★

One of the most popular series ever published for young Americans, these classics have been praised alike by parents, teachers, and librarians. With these lively, inspiring, fictionalized biographies—easily read by children of eight and up—today's youngster is swept right into history.

ABIGAIL ADAMS ★ JOHN ADAMS ★ LOUISA MAY ALCOTT ★ SUSAN B. ANTHONY ★ NEIL ARMSTRONG ★ CRISPUS ATTUCKS ★ CLARA BARTON ★ ELIZABETH BLACKWELL ★ DANIEL BOONE ★ BUFFALO BILL ★ ROBERTO CLEMENTE ★ DAVY CROCKETT ★ JOE DIMAGGIO ★ WALT DISNEY ★ AMELIA EARHART ★ THOMAS A. EDISON ★ ALBERT EINSTEIN ★ HENRY FORD ★ BENJAMIN FRANKLIN ★ LOU GEHRIG ★ GERONIMO ★ ALTHEA GIBSON ★ JOHN GLENN ★ JIM HENSON ★ HARRY HOUDINI ★ LANGSTON HUGHES ★ ANDREW JACKSON ★ MAHALIA JACKSON ★ THOMAS JEFFERSON ★ HELEN KELLER ★ JOHN FITZGERALD KENNEDY ★ MARTIN LUTHER KING JR. ★ ROBERT E. LEE ★ MERIWETHER LEWIS ★ ABRAHAM LINCOLN ★ MARY TODD LINCOLN ★ THURGOOD MARSHALL ★ JOHN MUIR ★ ANNIE OAKLEY ★ JACQUELINE KENNEDY ONASSIS ★ ROSA PARKS ★ MOLLY PITCHER ★ POCAHONTAS ★ RONALD REAGAN ★ PAUL REVERE ★ JACKIE ROBINSON ★ KNUTE ROCKNE ★ MR. ROGERS ★ ELEANOR ROOSEVELT ★ FRANKLIN DELANO ROOSEVELT ★ TEDDY ROOSEVELT ★ BETSY ROSS ★ WILMA RUDOLPH ★ BABE RUTH ★ SACAGAWEA ★ SITTING BULL ★ JIM THORPE ★ HARRY S. TRUMAN ★ SOJOURNER TRUTH ★ HARRIET TUBMAN ★ MARK TWAIN ★ GEORGE WASHINGTON ★ MARTHA WASHINGTON ★ LAURA INGALLS WILDER ★ WILBUR AND ORVILLE WRIGHT

★ ★ ★ Collect them all! ★ ★ ★